ESSENTIAL
MANAGEMENT

ESSENTIAL MANAGEMENT

Approaches and Practices for Line and HR Leaders in Turbulent Times

Ronald Gribbins, MBA, Ph.D.,
Mary Ruzicka, MBA, SHRM-SCP, CCP,
Lisa Youngdahl, MA, SPHR, SHRM-SCP

Charleston, SC
www.PalmettoPublishing.com

Essential Management

Copyright © 2023 by Ron Gribbins, Mary Ruzicka, and Lisa Youngdahl

All rights reserved

No portion of this book may be reproduced, stored in a retrieval system, or transmitted in any form by any means—electronic, mechanical, photocopy, recording, or other—except for brief quotations in printed reviews, without prior permission of the author.

First Edition

Hardcover ISBN: 979-8-8229-1096-6
Paperback ISBN: 979-8-8229-1097-3
eBook ISBN: 979-8-8229-1098-0

Dedication

To our students, one and all

Contents

Introduction 1
General Management Section
    Leadership 6
    Strategy 15
    Decision-Making 22
    Motivation 34
    Culture 45
    Change Management (Transformational) 49
Human Resources Management (HRM) Section 59
    Scope of the Work for HR 62
    The Selection Process 63
    Compensation 72
    Performance Management 79
    Termination/Separation 87
    Change Management (Transactional) 94
    Conclusion 107
Glossary 113
Acknowledgments 115
Permissions 116
Bibliography 117

Introduction

"Management is not rocket science. It is much more difficult." This statement (author unknown) is utilized in many different disciplines and is frequently used when someone is considering the complexities encountered in the management arena.

So why is management so difficult to execute? There are lots of reasons:

1. Management occurs in a very dynamic and complex context.
2. Management involves people who are very unpredictable and complex.
3. The pace of change continues at a substantially increased rate.
4. The time to reflect and consider all alternatives is a thing of the past.
5. There are lots of variables to consider, and they do not occur in a sequential fashion. Often, the variables feed back on each other. They are looped. More on this concept later.

There is another more chronic situation that makes managing difficult: there is a large gap between the day-in and day-out activity of on-the-job managerial behavior and the more academic fields that support the world of management. Some label it as the town versus gown perspective. This gap has been in existence for centuries.

For our purposes, individual managers see a problem and they either jump in to repair it or they look for the person who is responsible and have that individual address the problem. Academics step back to gain a greater understanding of the context and the many elements that may be contributing to the issue. Before long there is the beginning of a new theory that addresses the situation. Managers operate in the here and now at the five-foot level. Academics typically operate at the twenty-thousand-foot level. This is clearly an oversimplification of the differences, but it does characterize the gap.

Consider another perspective. When you typically study management, the content of management is laid out in very discrete and detailed pieces (accounting, finance, marketing, supply chain management, organizational behavior, etc.). Equal effort is not expended to put these functional areas together in a unified whole. On the other hand, the challenges of management are not encountered in the discrete pieces you typically studied in the functional disciplines. Moreover, the actions that you may propose in a case study do not have real consequences attached to them, so your feet are not held to the fire as happens in real life.

Real management is like taking a drink off a fire hose. You have two choices: one is to take a drink off the side and watch the left or right cheek of your face become quickly ripped off. The other alternative is to jump in front of the fire hose and drink *fast*. This will not work either. You are quickly impaled against the back wall. Real management also encounters most, if not all, of its variables simultaneously.

Management should be viewed as a marathon, not a sprint. Some actions may be taken in the present, but they then become part of the fabric of the organization and may rear their ugly heads later on. Striking a balance between the short and long term is critical to the long-term sustainability of the organization.

Here are the objectives of this book. We hope you will learn to separate the wheat from the chaff surrounding the process of management and:

Focus on essential activities of line and human resources management that confront the practicing leader.

1. Address the here and now but be aware of the implications that management activity has for the long run.

2. Use models to assist in focusing on the important elements of the management challenge and learn how these models may make the challenge of management less onerous. The need for more effective management has never been more pressing than it is today. Executing it correctly will save lots of pain.
3. Be very sensitive to the fact that organizations are not linear and sequential. Frequently, the management activities are looped. If the HR department sees that the firm is fully staffed, it will reduce additional recruiting activities. The firm seeks a balance between its desired situation and the actions that might increase or decrease various levels beyond what is judged to be optimal. These are loops. Organizations are full of these loops. Some are simple but many are very complex. Accepting this perspective will tend to reduce confusion.
4. Provide paths to consider, not answers. If the reader improves his or her analytical and critical thinking skills in the course of reading this text, success is achieved. The problems encountered in the future will require new answers. Learning to think more critically will move the ball forward.
5. Be a strong advocate for systems thinking.

The tendency is for one to focus on the here and now and to take a more departmental or divisional focus. Certainly, the organizational reward systems tend to promote this focus. Many elements contribute to managerial effectiveness. The objective here is to provide an overview of the essential management elements within the context of a systems perspective. It is our view that this will significantly improve the execution of management behavior.

And what are the essential elements? This book discusses the following essential elements:

Line Management
- Leadership
- Strategy
- Motivation
- Decision-Making
- Change Management (transformational)

HR Management
- Selection
- Compensation
- Performance Management
- Termination
- Change Management (transactional)

The changes in your behavior will not occur overnight. Consider these essential activities as a base:

- Immersing yourself in reality
- Exercising your critical and analytical skills
- Seeking out models that assist in explaining what is observed
- Facilitating the identification and execution of effective interventions
- Maintaining a balance between the short and long run
- Employing systems thinking

Each one will make you a more efficient and effective manager. Who should read this text?

1. The person considering a career in management
2. The individual who has just accepted a management position
3. Current middle managers who think, "There must be a better way"

4. People who do not have all the answers
5. People who are willing to do some self-reflection
6. People who are willing to grow
7. Top management, because they need to support all the others in their quest to do it better
8. Top management, because they still have some things to learn

The topics covered in this text do not lend themselves to quick and clear answers. In many instances, you encounter tradeoffs, and the actions eventually taken are not necessarily optimal. If you live to see another day, that may be viewed as progress. In some instances, you will be presented with some questions at the end of the section that require reflection and further reading. Take time to smell the roses and enjoy the journey.

Leadership

Leadership is clearly an important topic for organizational life. The only problem is that choosing the right approach is extremely difficult. A search on Amazon for "leadership" netted sixty thousand books. You read that correctly: sixty thousand entries. Getting this number down to a more manageable list is the order of the day. That said, are there some lessons that are decent takeaways for leading an organization in today's turbulent times? To be fair, the management literature has pursued three avenues to keep in mind.

1. Traits: Is there a reasonable number of traits associated with effective leadership? Lots of effort is expended here, but there are few successful lists. If a list is still called for, the following may help: intelligence, good interpersonal skills, integrity, humor, and self-initiative.

    Intelligence is not measured by the number of degrees you have; it is better to think of intelligence as common sense. Lots of communication goes on in an organization, which makes this an important managerial trait. One colleague expressed it in this manner: "You need to be able to tell an individual to go to hell in such a fashion that he is looking forward to taking the trip." Crude but insightful.

    Integrity is essential. If trust is not found in abundance in the organization, then the end is in sight.

    Humor is very important, and you'd better be able to laugh at yourself for a good start.

    Finally, self-initiative is very important. Failure is inevitable. The question is what you do with failure. Look at it as a

learning experience and hold on to the lessons learned. Fear of failure is not a good leadership trait.
2. Behaviors: Is there a significant difference between autocratic, participative, instrumental, and laissez-faire approaches to leadership in terms of outcome effectiveness? Yes, but... These "buts" move us into various contingency approaches to leadership.
3. Contingencies: So what are the contingencies that should be considered? Leader-member relations, task structure, position power, etc.? There is something to be said for the various contingency approaches, but there are lots of them.

We are going to explore one of these contingency approaches primarily because:

1. It takes a systematic approach and offers several feedback loops that make the model suitable with the current global situation.
2. It offers an important balance among leadership traits and behaviors and the other variables included within the model.
3. It focuses on processes that must be fostered for leadership to be effective.
4. It recognizes that the development of the various processes is not accomplished in the short term. These processes take time and effort to develop, to grow, and to improve.

The Leadership Process Model, proposed by Dunham and Pierce, is the model of choice.

DUNHAM & PIERCE LEADERSHIP PROCESS MODEL

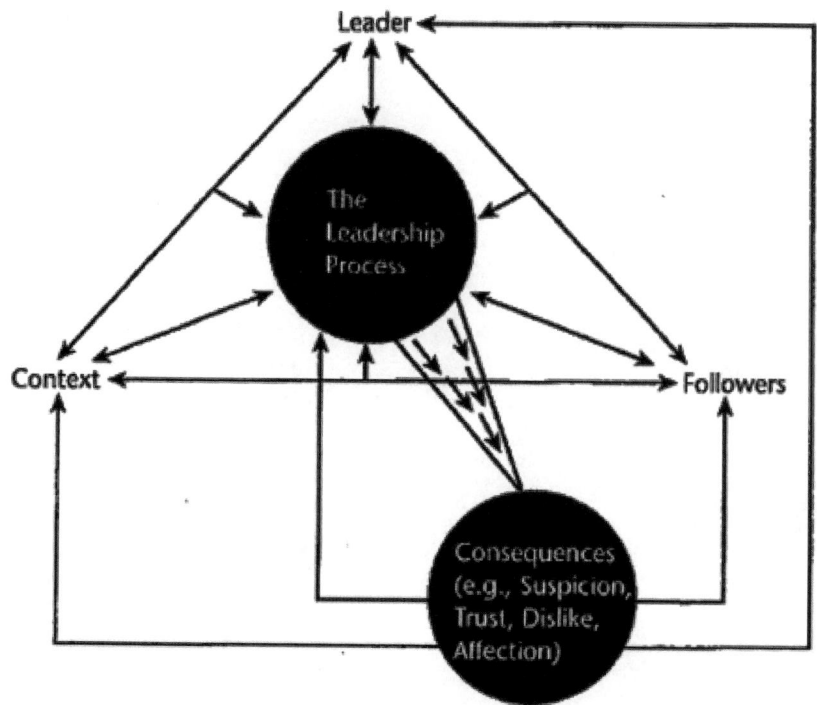

Dunham and Pierce employ four elements: Leader, Followers, Context, and Outcomes. Their goal is to explain how these factors interact for the long-term effectiveness of the organization. The focus on the long term is critical. There are few factors to consider, but it is important to remember that attention to these variables is not conducted in a sequential manner. It is imperative to recognize that attention must be devoted to all the variables within a concurrent approach. It may be that a more developmental approach among the variables may be most effective in the long run.

The Sequence of Relationships

> - Leader and Followers. This is the model's primary link, and the relationship is looped. To say the relationship is looped is to say that the two variables influence each other and the influence can

be either positive or negative. For example, the manager may provide clear expectations regarding what he wants the subordinate to accomplish. The subordinate follows the marching orders and accomplishes the task with very good outcomes. The subordinate's confidence goes up and he also has a more positive feeling toward the boss. The manager sees the positive performance and his confidence in the subordinate continues to improve. This is an example of the feedback loop and it is positive.

On the other hand, the boss may micro-manage the subordinate. The subordinate feels the manager does not trust him to accomplish the task on his own and the relationship between boss and subordinate does not improve. Eventually, the subordinate starts looking for a new job. In this instance the loop is still there but it is negative. The looped nature of organizational life is everywhere. It can be with colleagues, departments and even organizations.

The leader invests in the followers through training and coaching with clear attention given to accomplishing the task. Over time, if the job is accomplished successfully, the level of trust among all parties grows. On the other hand, the positive results are easily lost if the leader chews out a follower in a manner that is deemed inappropriate by the followers. Be in control of your own emotions and be a good role model for the other members of the team.

➢ Job performance is not accomplished in a vacuum. It occurs within a larger context including other groups of followers, various departments, and then the multitude of factors that the organization must consider as it addresses its short- and long-term objectives. These are all included in the Context. The Context influences both the Leader and the Followers. Providing encouragement to the followers that a task can be accomplished is both a confidence builder and an opportunity to learn additional skills. Proceed openly and ethically, and beneficial outcomes will generally occur. Typically, effective leadership is a skill developed over time. This is a marathon, not a sprint. Secure the foundation with strong teams, and the firm will be in a good position to withstand the larger assaults to its existence.

The Leader and Followers may have substantial influence over some parts of the Context, but the external Context probably has more influence over the Leader and Followers than the other way around.

➤ If the Leader and Followers address the Context in a thoughtful and balanced manner, it is expected that this Leadership Process will typically lead to expected Outcomes that foster organizational sustainability and survival.

➤ If expected Outcomes are not achieved, all four of the variables in the model are linked through loops that foster after-action review and then further planning for the next business cycle.

Another systematic approach, still focusing on the leadership issue, more fully develops the various "Action Logics" exhibited by leaders, and it also provides a significant insight to all organizations and practicing leaders. Action logics (Rooke and Torbert) employs a Leadership Development Profile to determine which style is dominant for an individual. They studied thousands of practicing leaders and identified the following action logics.

The list below presents the styles from least to most effective:

Opportunist: they view their behavior as legitimate, are not open to much feedback, like to be in control, and treat others as competitors.

Diplomat: they tend to avoid conflict. Change is difficult for them. Others will take advantage of them.

Expert: logic and expertise will carry the day. They like to work alone. Collaboration is a waste of time.

Achiever: they can take the strategic plan and translate it into actionable goals. They are supportive of others and enjoy a pleasant work environment.

Individualist: they strike a balance between strategy and performance. Potential conflict is a source of excitement.

Strategist: this individual accomplishes both organizational and individual transformations. The individual does not shy away from conflict and intense debate. The strategist works well with change.

Alchemist: this individual can generate social transformations. He/she integrates material, spiritual, and social transformations.

The challenge is that Rooke and Torbert find these seven action logics exhibited in the following percentages:

Opportunist	5 percent
Diplomat	12 percent
Expert	38 percent
Achiever	30 percent
Individualist	10 percent
Strategist	4 percent
Alchemist	1 percent

Note that the alchemist, their most effective action logic, is possessed by only 1 percent of their sample of practicing managers.

Things to Think About
For the individual:
1. Determine your action logic
2. Do you wish to transform into another Action Logic?
3. How will you accomplish this?

For the organization:
1. What is the percentage distribution within your firm?
2. What implications does this distribution have for talent acquisition and career development? Rooke and Torbert employ a Leadership Development Profile to determine which style is dominant for an individual. Use this analytical technique to provide a baseline for the organization and then develop strategies to improve the situation.

It is also important to have a realistic view of how effective leaders do their job. Consider three approaches to this question.

1. The leader accomplishes his or her work directly. The leader decides the goal to be accomplished and then goes after it by determining the strategy, assembling the necessary resources, assigning tasks to individual employees, coordinating the work, and monitoring the job until the goal is reached.
2. The second approach dictates that the leader accomplishes the goal through his or her key associates, who then manage the process through their various team members. The leader checks with the key associates to make sure all is in order.
3. The third approach looks to the team as the essential body that gets the job done. Consider the CEO and the senior management team as an example. The CEO ensures that all members of the senior management team are competent in their specific roles and work effectively across functions with those individuals who lead those individual functions. This approach to leadership can also work throughout the organization. If implemented effectively, it provides more degrees of freedom to those in leadership roles to address the strategic issues facing the firm as a whole by delegating the more operational activities to those charged with managing these tasks.

The three diagrams portray these three approaches.

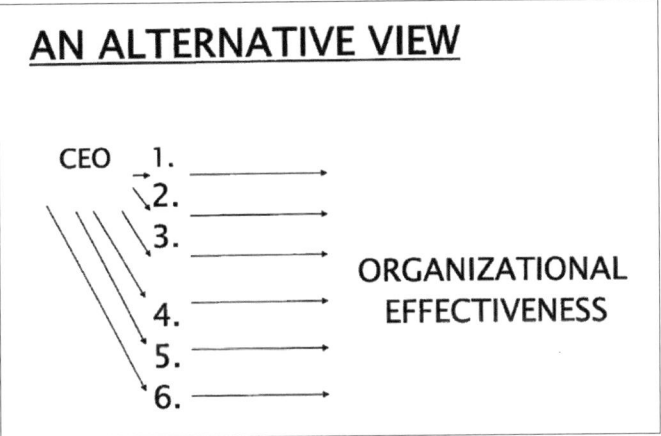

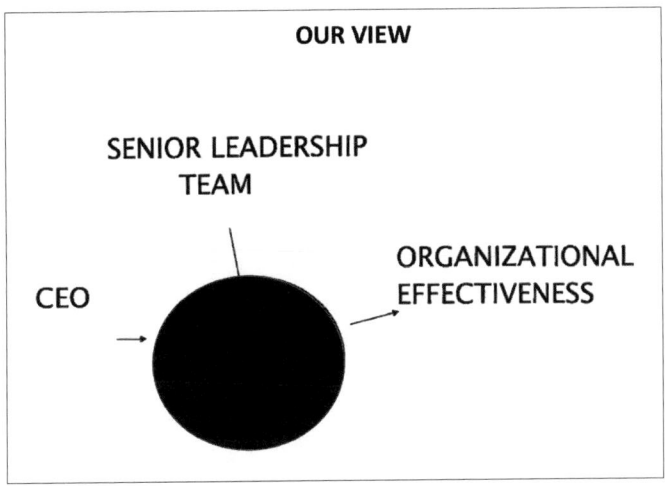

Rest assured that there is overlap within these three approaches. A laudable objective for leadership to achieve is when the team below the leader makes the observation that "We did it ourselves." Mission accomplished.

Strategy

If you don't know where you are going, any road can take you there.
—The Cheshire Cat

You've got to be very careful if you don't know where you are going, because you might not get there.
—Yogi Berra

It is very easy for organizations to ignore the focus on strategy. If the firm is relatively small and/or relatively new, current problems frequently drive out thinking about strategy. If the organization is large and/or established, it continues along the path it has been on. The organization has the resources to ignore the changes in the marketplace. If the firm has been successful, it might not even see the changes that are occurring in the marketplace because management is simply not looking for change trends.

This section considers the topic of strategy by examining examples of mission statements and then building an approach to strategy formation that ensures the mission remains relevant and guides further growth in the organization.

Mission Statements

#1   The Chocolate Shoppe in Madison, Wisconsin
*"Don't even ask. This is the best ice cream made in Wisconsin, and it tastes so good because it has gobs of rich Wisconsin cream, tons of real ingredients for **boatloads** of luscious flavors. That means it's not low-fat, low-calorie, or low anything, and that's why everyone loves it. You want nutrition, eat carrots."*

As you enter the Chocolate Shoppe on State Street in Madison, Wisconsin, you find many pictures and posters on the walls and the "mission statement" quoted above. A few observations:

1. The majority of people that enter the store have read that statement at one time or another. Its location on the walls occasionally changes but the message has been the same for the umpteen years I have been going there.

   The Chocolate Shoppe was there when I was a graduate student in the early seventies at the University of Wisconsin, and the shop is still going strong today. As a tangent, give a shout out to the Parthenon for its longevity as another State Street operation. It still provides the best damn gyro sandwich in the Midwest. Few State Street operations have lasted this long.
2. What is your guess concerning who wrote the mission statement for the Chocolate Shoppe? My guess is that the owner wrote it.
3. There is no question as to what the shop is about. Read the statement and deliver on the promise.

#2   Babson College in Wellesley, Massachusetts

"Babson College prepares and empowers entrepreneurial leaders who create, grow and steward sustainable economic and social value—everywhere."

Eighteen words say it all!

Babson is a small college, but the Business School has been ranked #1 in the nation in Entrepreneurial Management for twenty-six years in a row. The college has approximately 3,300 students. A few observations:

1. Who do you think wrote this mission statement? My bet is that a faculty committee drafted the statement and then it was approved by the Board of Trustees.

2. How does a college with 3,300 students maintain its #1 ranking in the nation for entrepreneurial management for twenty-six years straight? Competition in this space is substantial, and many of Babson's competitors are much larger. Babson College does not attempt to be all things to all people. It has chosen a very specific niche and remains focused on being the best provider of that curriculum in the nation.

    It also employs a partnering approach with like-minded institutions across the globe. It teams up with other institutions and then students can take courses at these institutions and apply them to degree requirements at Babson. This approach is mentioned below when discussing vehicles.

#3   Washington University in St. Louis, Missouri

"Washington University in St. Louis' mission is to discover and disseminate knowledge, and protect the freedom of inquiry through research, teaching and learning. Washington University creates an environment to encourage and support an ethos of wide-ranging exploration. Washington University's faculty and staff strive to enhance the lives and livelihoods of students, the people of the greater St. Louis community, the country and the world."

1. This is a very balanced mission statement and covers all fronts. The question is: who wrote the mission statement? My bet is that the public relations department prepared the mission statement, and it was then reviewed and adopted by the Board of Trustees.
2. This mission statement, like the majority of university mission statements, is very balanced and comprehensive, but these are not statements that students and faculty memorize and carry around for quick reference. They lack the focus seen in the first two examples.

Effective mission statements are focused and create alignment for the institution. If you pet a cat, try going from the tail to the head. The cat will be on its way immediately. Pet the cat from head to tail and the cat will stay around for more. The fur is aligned.

Models

So how do you develop an effective mission statement that aligns all the organization's resources? This is the point at which frameworks or models provide relevant assistance. There are many books on the topic of strategy, and you can even take full courses devoted to the topic. The model recommended here comes from an article by Donald Hambrick and James Fredrickson entitled "Are you sure you have a strategy?"

Their model considers five key elements. If the questions these elements raise are answered, you have a strategy.

1. Arenas

    What are the products or services the organization offers?
    Who is the target market?

2. Vehicles

    Does the organization have all the needed resources in-house?

    Is it necessary for the organization to purchase another firm that has a resource lacking in the first organization? (i.e., a merger)

    Does the firm intend to joint venture with other organizations in pursuit of its goals?

3. Differentiators

    How does the organization differentiate itself from other organizations in the same market? Is Nordstrom different in the way it makes itself appealing to the intended customer? Go to a Walmart Supercenter, then Costco, and then the neighborhood supermarket, and note the differences.

Who is the intended customer? How are the products presented? What is the range of products available? These three organizations have many of the same products, but they have a unique feel. Each has differentiated itself from its competitors.

4. Staging

In the planning process, it quickly becomes apparent that the organization cannot accomplish all needed projects immediately. It becomes necessary to ask: Where do we want to be in five years, and what needs to be accomplished in year one to move the firm in that direction? What needs to happen in year two and so on down the line?

Rigorous review on a yearly basis is needed to ensure appropriate progress. Markets change and the organization is changing. Regular review and plan updates are necessary.

5. Economic Logic

The first three elements cluster together to answer the marketing agenda and the organizational resources needed to achieve the marketing plan. The fourth element details the specific steps needed in real time to meet the long-term goal(s). Economic logic asks the hard questions: Does this plan ensure that the organization will make a dollar? Will achieving the plan produce expected revenues? Ask these questions.

If all five factors are answered to the satisfaction of the strategic planning group, then the organization has a strategy.

Tools

It is highly recommended that the organization employ a skilled facilitator to guide the team through this exercise. The facilitator keeps all parties focused and makes sure the agenda is followed. The big advantage in using a facilitator is that he or she has no vested interest in the deliberations and outcomes.

Here too, there are several tools available to the strategic planning group. A widely used approach is to start with a review of where the organization currently stands by employing a SWOT analysis. The SWOT analysis asks, what are the Strengths and Weaknesses of the organization? These two questions focus on the organization. The next two focus externally. What are the Opportunities for the organization and what are the Threats to consider?

The SWOT analysis provides a foundation for the planning group by anchoring the deliberations in reality. When this is accomplished, the group can then turn to the five factors noted above to begin to address the strategy process. Once the five factors have been reviewed and answered, it is important to assess and choose the three to five action plans that will be addressed in the next year as the first steps in meeting the five-year plan.

These action plans should be stated as goals that employ the SMART format.

1. Are the goals Specific?
2. Are the goals Measurable?
3. Are the goals Achievable?
4. Are the goals Relevant?
5. Are the goals Timely?

Finally, which individual or team is accountable for meeting the goal(s)?

This process, employed on annual basis, will significantly contribute to aligning the organization by developing specific goals and determining who is accountable for their accomplishment.

It is important to note that a specific five-year goal has not been recommended. It is our belief that:

1. It is very difficult to articulate a meaningful five-year plan in the current environment. The external environment is too dynamic and too complex to state a five-year goal.
2. If the process suggested here is employed, the organization will have an aligned direction that is more than capable of bending as the situation (both internal and external) dictates.

Decision-Making

A good decision is based on knowledge, and not on numbers.
—Plato

A bedrock of management thinking is that a rational approach to decision-making nets both efficient and effective decisions for the organization and its stakeholders. The rational decision model (not my favorite) consists of the following steps:

1. Identify the problem or opportunity.
2. Gather relevant information.
3. Analyze the situation.
4. Develop options.
5. Evaluate the options.
6. Select the preferred option.
7. Implement the decision.

There are also important assumptions that are included in this model.

1. The decision-maker has full and perfect information on which to base a decision. This should be a big red flag for anyone tasked with the decision-making responsibility. The business environment and, for that matter, the entire global environment is very complex and dynamic. Attempting to maintain a reasonable handle on this situation is well-nigh impossible. The idea that you have perfect information about macro influences affecting the organization calls for a big leap of faith.

2. Measurable criteria exist on which data can be collected and analyzed. Again, lots to consider here. For example, the organization can measure voluntary turnover fairly readily. Two precursors to voluntary turnover, employee engagement and job satisfaction, are more difficult to measure accurately.
3. The decision-maker has the wherewithal to evaluate the alternatives and make a decision. Doubt it.

Oh, that it were this easy. Meeting the assumptions of the rational decision approach makes this model difficult to employ appropriately in many of the decision-making situations encountered in the organization. This chapter is not about to boil the ocean and discuss all the factors facing the organization's decision-makers. The goal here is to convey a general understanding of the process of decision-making and position the interested reader in the right direction to pose further questions and search for appropriate answers. The process will consider several essential contingencies and then explore decision-making approaches that may facilitate effective decision-making in that circumstance.

To start, there are several different categories of decision-making situations within an organization, and they are by no means homogeneous. These situations are closely aligned with the decision-making levels of the firm.

1. Strategic: Members of the top management team are constantly grappling with the strategic and long-term issues for their departments and, as members of the senior level, participating in the development and execution of the strategic plan for the organization. This situation is highly unstructured due to the ambiguity, uncertainty, and dynamics confronting the decision-makers. Several problems might emerge: (1) the team

has difficulty framing the situation and setting reasonable steps to measure plan progress; (2) new members to the top management team lack organizational history; (3) the planning process becomes quagmired in the mud and then, in frustration, the leader makes a command decision to simply rescue the team from the mud pit. This situation calls for a style that is sensitive to the uncertainties faced and provides a more tentative approach to the problem.

2. Tactical: Members of the middle management team often are tasked with implementing action plans that result from the strategic planning process. Middle managers do not possess the line authority to force a decision. They have authority within their department but need to influence the decision-making process through reason and persuasion when interacting with fellow department heads involved in accomplishing the action plans. The politics of organizational life can become severe. Scapegoating, finger pointing, and backpedaling strategies carry the day. The command decision will not work. Like it or not, consultation and participation are frequently needed to gain better understanding and acceptance of the path that is finally chosen for implementing the action plans.

3. Operational: Employees who are doing the day-in and day-out activities associated with production are typically the unsung heroes and manage the many routine processes and procedures needed to get the job done. In many instances, this work is executed by robotic machinery. The decision-making processes surrounding this work lend themselves to more rational decision-making processes because of the standardization inherent in the work and the capacity to measure various goals which leads to greater optimization.

The First Perspective Framework: Incrementalism

An approach that lends itself well to the considerations noted above is Incrementalism. The original formulation of this approach is found in an important article by Charles Lindblom entitled "The Science of Muddling Through." It appeared in the *Public Administration Review* in 1959. The intended audience was governmental employees, but it has direct relevance to what is encountered in any business entity today. The title alone provides a very good insight to what is envisioned. It is presented in five contrasts.

1. The rational approach would explore the values held dear by the organization. Once the review of values has occurred and all are on board, the group would then move to solving the problem. The muddling through approach recognizes the complexities and uncertainties enmeshed in the problem and opts for a more limited set of values and alternatives. For example, the university's top management team is convinced that hiring outstanding faculty will solve everything. Better students will eventually apply, more prestigious firms will recruit there, and more money will flow to the university's endowment. All is good. As another example, an auto company believes that the quality of the car produced will carry the day. The marketing budget is lowered, the training of the sales force takes a significant hit, etc.
2. The rational approach opts for a means-ends analysis. The muddling through approach argues that means and ends are not distinct. Producing a high-quality auto is both an end and a mean. Lots of tail chasing can ensue.
3. The test for the value of a decision is framed simply: does it maximize the desired outcome? Now, for the tricky part. The muddling through approach states that dueling parties can agree on

a decision without considering conflicting goals. An example will help. The parties are arguing the merits of two approaches that are diametrically opposed to each other. As the time draws near to end the meeting, someone proposes that a committee be formed to study the issue in more detail. Team A likes the idea because it believes that the committee will finally get to the bottom of the issue and resolve it in Team A's favor. Team B members are more cynical. This committee will go the way of many committees, and there will never be a report. The routine activities of the day drive out the nonroutine activities of deliberating on a committee. Team B likes the idea because this will kill the idea. Cynical? Yes. Typical? Also yes. The committee is formed.

4. The rational approach is comprehensive in its deliberations. The muddling through approach is drastically limited. For example, take the issue of how much of an increase in retail price should be implemented for a car line next year. The rational approach would have a task force of accountants determining the costs associated with all expenses and proceed accordingly. The muddling through approach would increase the price a bit and see what happens. If the sales volume is not affected negatively, corporate would raise the price again the next year.

5. The rational approach relies heavily on theory, while the incremental approach operates by a succession of comparisons. The incremental approach does not invest a great deal in the current decision. If it works, great; if it doesn't, discard it and try another approach. This type of flexibility is nice to have available to decision-makers in times of great uncertainty.

Incrementalism has significant relevance at the strategic level and probably spills over to tactical decisions. The approach may seem sloppy and lazy, but its strength is that it fits the situation faced and is flexible.

The Second Perspective Framework: Quality, Acceptance, and Save Time

Decision-making in the operational space is relatively certain because the goals are known and how they are to be accomplished becomes more standardized over time. Initially, there was likely a serious amount of trial and error with a clear objective of making the accomplishment of the goal both efficient and effective. The technology (what must be done to get the job done) is dynamic. Advances are continual, and these must be integrated into the flow of the work. The issue of quality is very important because time is money and identifying a very efficient way of doing the job takes first place. What frequently happens, however, is that the decision-maker fails to address the fact that individuals on the line are doing the work and he is not one of these individuals. Their buy-in to the process is essential for long-term effectiveness. Finally, the goal of saving time is also an important consideration. The issue then becomes: (1) when can the manager make an autocratic decision, (2) when does the manager need to consult with those who are doing the work, and (3) when does the manager let the team make the decision?

There is a system proposed by Victor Vroom and Phillip Yetton that answers these three questions and provides an initial road map to follow. They provide a list of seven rules and then a decision tree that incorporates these rules and assists the manager in choosing the appropriate decision-making model of the three mentioned: (1) make the decision yourself (autocratic), (2) consult with those affected by the decision but maintain final decision-making authority (consultative), or (3) let the team determine the decision (participative).

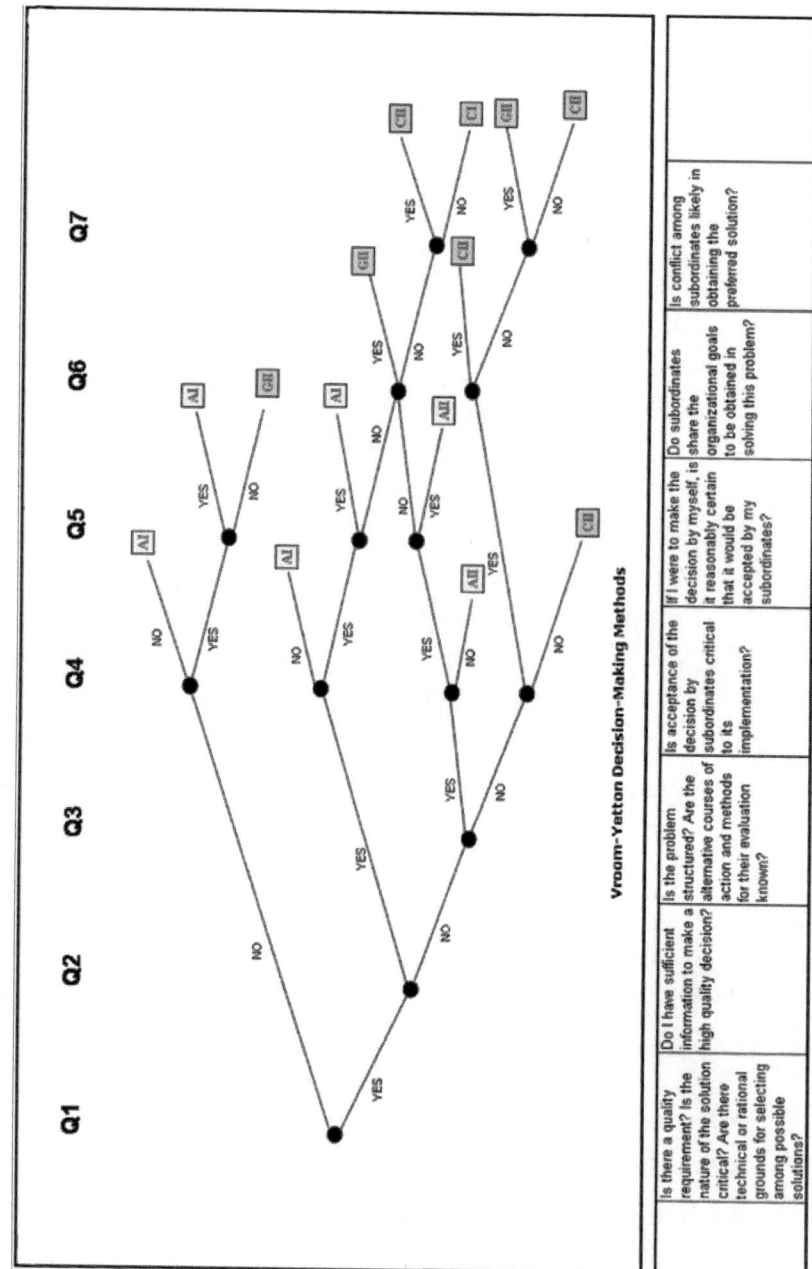

Consider the following problem confronting a manager. A new piece of machinery and related processes have been introduced into a rival company like the one considered here. Productivity is increasing and profits are continuing to grow in that other organization. The manager is about to pull the trigger and introduce the system in his organization. However, he remembers attending a session on decision-making at a recent professional meeting he attended. He decides he will give it a try. He pulls out the decision tree and proceeds to ask himself the appropriate questions.

- Question #1: Is there a quality requirement? In other words, is there one solution that is likely to be better than all the rest? His answer to the question is "Yes." All he has to do is figure out which of several competing alternatives is the best.
- Question #2: Does he have sufficient information to make the decision? Well, he thinks he does, but then he has not worked a position on the line in twenty years. Besides, lots has changed since he was on the line. His answer is "No."
- Question #3: Is the problem structured? This is an assembly line operation. The product comes down the line and the employees add parts to the product and then do some quality assessment to ensure the product is working correctly. The answer to question #3 is "Yes."
- Question #4: Is acceptance of the decision by subordinates critical to implementation? The manager is not on the line, subordinates are. If they don't like the new system, regardless of why, problems are on the horizon. Work slowdown and even sabotage are a couple of immediate ones. Maybe the new system would call for skills the current employees do not have. He answers question #4 with a reluctant "Yes."
- Question #5: If I make the decision, is it reasonably certain that the employees would accept the decision? Welcome to the slippery slope. "He has not been on the line in years." "He rarely stops by to say hello." The subordinates observe "We do the

work, and he gets the big paycheck." All are frequent statements heard on the line. And so on. The manager begins to think they may not be very accepting of the decision if he makes it. Eventually, the manager decides the answer to the question is "No."

- Question #6: Do subordinates share the organizational goals? "I think so" is the immediate response. On second thought, the employees may simply be interested in the paycheck. They like the organization and hope it succeeds because it provides a job. Little else concerns them. He answers "Yes."

- Question #7: Is conflict among the employees possible? Well, there is a lot of diversity on the line: age, race, and gender are a few factors. All have different opinions about what should be happening on the line. Issues related to equity, career development, and advancement could all enter into the discussion. If the answer to Question #6 is "Yes," the decision matrix suggests that the manager meet with the employees as a group and consult with them about the new production system. Consultation provides the opportunity to hear all sides and even their recommendation, but final decision-making authority rests with the manager.

Employing this decision tree will probably decrease the number of times a manager employs an authoritarian style. This approach may take longer, but many potential pitfalls are avoided in the process. The diagram is a useful framework for initiating the decision-making process. It will not answer all problems. Keep the diagram in the top drawer of the desk, but keep in mind the Three Envelope story. The new managerial hire is meeting with his predecessor, who gives him three envelopes before departing. His guidance is to keep these envelopes in the drawer and take one out when a problem emerges that has the boss in big trouble with no solutions readily available. He thanks him but says, "I don't think I will need them." Nine months later, he is in deep trouble and does not know what to do. He then remembers the three envelopes in the desk drawer. He takes the first one out and opens it. The message says, "Blame it on the prior manager." It carries the day, and everything returns to normal.

Twelve months later, another major problem confronts the manager. He returns to the desk and takes out the second envelope. The message reads, "Blame it on the system." He does, and he is off the hook. Two years later, another problem emerges and there seems to be no answer in sight. He goes to the desk and takes out the third envelope. He opens it and the message says, "Prepare three envelopes."

The Third Perspective: The Eisenhower Decision Matrix

A frequently observed condition, one of many, is that the decision-maker procrastinates. The problem will not go away, and the more procrastination that takes place the more urgent the problem becomes. Another condition is that the decision-maker is focused on an unimportant issue. Both are dysfunctional behaviors. The Eisenhower decision matrix is worth your attention.

This is a very useful tool to help a frazzled manager get his or her ducks in order. It was developed by former U.S. President Dwight Eisenhower, who certainly had to make monumental decisions in a very quick and effective manner.

There are two dimensions associated with this matrix.

1. Is the situation you face urgent or nonurgent?
2. Is the issue to be addressed important or not important?

	URGENT	NONURGENT
IMPORTANT	Do something now	Schedule time to address it
NOT IMPORTANT	Delegate the activity to someone else	Ignore or dismiss

Urgent and important activities can include picking up the kids at school, responding to critical emails, finishing a project report, etc.

Nonurgent and important activities may include strategic planning, professional development, personal exercising, etc.

Urgent and not important activities may include scheduling and coordinating an important event, etc.

Nonurgent and not important activities include playing solitaire, reading all the junk mail, picking up the phone when you are almost sure it is a solicitor, etc.

An easily actionable recommendation is to write down the problems you are confronting until their placement on the matrix becomes second nature, and then act accordingly.

Do, Plan, Delegate, Dismiss

Do, Schedule, Delegate, Eliminate

CONCLUSION

Modeling appropriate decision-making processes can have a beneficial effect on other members of the team. Decision-making is a huge topic because so many factors can be considered in the process. This chapter explored just a few.

1. At what level is the decision being made, and to what extent is the problem structured?
2. When is authoritarian decision-making appropriate, and when might consultative and/or participative decision-making be employed?
3. What can you do to improve your decision-making?

There are plenty of other avenues to pursue. A quick review of topics related to decision-making proves the point. Google results:

1. Emotion and decision-making
2. Feelings and decision-making
3. Humility and decision-making
4. Autocratic behavior and decision-making
5. Participative behavior and decision-making
6. Love and decision-making
7. Conflict and decision-making

The acquisition of decision-making skills is not a sprint; it is a marathon. Make a candid assessment as to how you currently make decisions and then develop a plan to gain the needed skills and attitudes to make more effective decisions in the future.

Motivation

Hire in haste, repent at leisure.
—Unknown

Strategy formation involves a set of activities that result in a path for aligning the organization and, hopefully, leading to long-term effectiveness and sustainability. It also provides a range of structural possibilities that make the efforts of fulfilling the strategy more or less reasonable. The questions surrounding the choice of an appropriate structure, while complex and frequently difficult, still focus on the choice of an optimal structure. The next area becomes much more complex. Management cannot do all the activities needed to implement the strategy. Management must employ additional employees.

These employees must be recruited, hired, trained, motivated, managed, evaluated, and, in many instances, promoted. The factors that must be considered and the questions that must be asked are too numerous to mention and involve many decisions that are less than optimal. Management at this point sees itself taking the proverbial drink off the fire hose.

Why do people work? That is the million-dollar question. The easy answer is that people work to make money. There are bills to pay, there are mouths to feed, and there is rent or a mortgage to be paid. Certainly, pay has been recognized as a key factor that people consider when looking at a particular job. However, there are many, many reasons why people work.

1. People work for pay.
2. People work for the health benefits the organization provides.
3. People work to make a difference in their community.

4. People work because they like the mission of the organization. This would be the case for many people who work for a not-for-profit organization.
5. People work to get out of the house.

And so on and so on. These barely scratch the surface. Obviously, there is not one simple answer to this very important question. Nevertheless, the organization needs employees to meet its agenda, and therefore talent acquisition becomes a major challenge early on in the life of the organization.

One thing is known: if the employee is satisfied on the job, he or she will typically remain on the job. If the employee sees that another organization has a similar job and is providing more positive outcomes valued by the employee, the employee will frequently resign from the current organization and take employment with the organization providing better outcomes.

How It Works

If the firm is young and employs few people, the human resource function frequently falls to the founder or the newly appointed president. If the organization has been in existence for a few years, the HR function may be delegated to the founder's assistant or maybe a newly minted HR generalist. Questions such as what role HR plays as a business partner, a change agent, and an employee champion (David Ulrich—Professor of Business at the University of Michigan) have yet to emerge

have yet to emerge. One might turn to Amazon for a book on motivation. Looking to Amazon for guidance is a daunting task. Type in "motivation" and you will find at least seventy thousand references. Two things are learned from this search.

First, motivation must be a very important activity to receive this much attention. Second, there are many opinions out there but very few hard and fast facts. In many management texts, the subject of motivation quickly moves to various theories that might provide clues to the interested reader. There are two main categories to consider: content approaches and process approaches. The two frequently cited content approaches are Abraham Maslow's Hierarchy of Needs and Fredrick Herzberg's Two-Factor approach.

For our purposes, we will leave the content approaches to the interested reader to pursue on his or her time. The focus of this chapter will be several interesting frames that are process approaches to the question of motivation. The discussion employed here will be an integration of several process approaches: Expectancy theory (Victor Vroom), Equity theory (Stacy Adams), Goal-setting theory (Edwin Locke) and Self-Determination theory (Edward Deci). The integrated picture is found later in this chapter. This discussion will consider several smaller parts independently and then present a more comprehensive framework for the question of motivation.

When the hiring manager seeks to employ someone, he or she typically has a position in mind that involves several activities and leads to an outcome called performance.

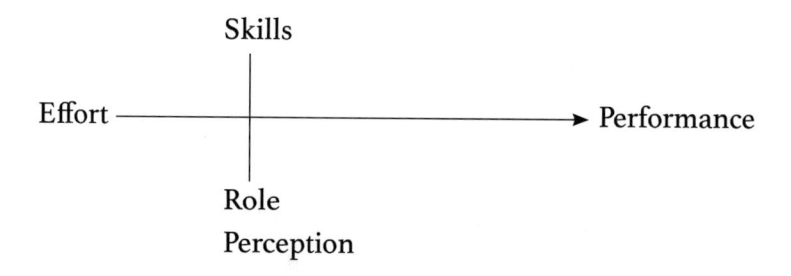

```
                  Skills
                    |
        Effort ─────┼─────▶ Performance
                    |
                  Role
                  Perception
```

The typical interview will focus primarily on assessing whether the candidate possesses the skills required to accomplish all the tasks needed leading to successful performance. An interviewer may also make a quick determination of whether the candidate will fit into the organization. This assessment is very subjective and can lead to many abuses and mistakes (more on this later). Numerous tests are readily available to assist in the skill assessment determination.

A second factor to consider is role perception. The candidate might expect that the job activities include "A" while the hiring manager's expectations are that the job involves "B." The job description helps to resolve these gaps. Early coaching opportunities between the newly hired individual and his or her boss seek to ensure that all parties agree on what is expected. The performance review is another opportunity to provide further clarification regarding what management expects regarding job performance. Many new hires engage in an orientation program with an experienced employee who helps in clarifying the job expectations and what is expected regarding performance outcomes.

The third factor in the graph above is effort. This is a measure of the work activity the individual puts into his or her job performance. There are many factors that are going to affect effort, but they come up later in this discussion, so we will pass for now. Suffice it to say that there are many individuals who have the skill needed to accomplish the task and a clear understanding of what they are supposed to do, but they simply do not initiate the activity needed to get the job done. For our purposes, then, all three of these factors need to work in concert to accomplish task performance.

There is another factor not indicated on the graph above that we need to consider. That factor is called "expectancy." Expectancy is a probability going from 0 to 1 that is held by the individual. He or she can look at a task and say it is an impossible task. In this instance, expectancy would be near zero. If the individual looks at the job to be performed and considers it very easy to accomplish, he or she would attach an expectancy of 1 to getting the job done. A very routine job will have an expectancy of something in the high .90 or better. Management can increase or decrease the expectancy held by the individual by the demands placed upon the individual. It is a very dynamic factor, and it can change quickly.

Job performance ⎯⎯⎯⎯⎯⎯⎯⎯⎯⎯→ Outcomes

Job performance leads to outcomes. The expectancy approach does not specify the outcomes of performance. It simply says that performance produces various outcomes. Some outcomes are perceived positively (positively valent) by the worker (pay or recognition, for example) and others are perceived as negative (negatively valent). Job stress or poor health due to working conditions are two examples. This approach leaves it to both management and the employee to determine what are the outcomes associated with acceptable performance on the job. The employee will look at all the positive outcomes of the job and also the negative outcomes and make a determination as to whether he or she wishes to engage in this job.

Management does not know, beforehand, what these positive and negative outcomes perceived by the employee are. The obvious conclusion is that management needs to ask the employee what the employee considers to be positive and negative outcomes. Further confounding this situation is the fact that several people executing the same job may have a different set of positive and negative outcomes associated with the job. As noted earlier, the motivation challenge is anything but simple. What is known is that dissatisfaction will typically lead to voluntary turnover.

There is another probability to consider here, and that is instrumentality. Instrumentality is defined as the belief that, if the employee accomplishes the performance expectations, he or she will receive the expected positive outcomes. For example, if you are a full-time employee, you would expect to find the paycheck deposited at the end of the month in your account. In this instance, pay would have an instrumentality of 1. An employee may also like to receive recognition for a job well done; however, the employee's boss is known for rarely passing out "attaboys" for a job well done. It may happen one in ten times. In this instance the instrumentality associated with a recognition from the boss would be .10. So for every outcome, positive or negative, there is a unique instrumentality attached to receiving the outcome.

Employee engagement is a theme touted today as a strategy for improving employee satisfaction. The Gallup survey results for 2020 recently found that nearly 20 percent of US employees were disengaged. Another 54 percent were neutral about their work. That means about 25 percent of employees are engaged and most probably satisfied in their work situation. Put another way, 50 percent of the employees are ready to leave the organization and are simply working to stay employed. They do their job, but that is about it. Another 20 percent are disengaged and may even be exhibiting dysfunctional behavior in their jobs. What would the effectiveness of the organization be if these 75 percent of the workforce were engaged and highly motivated?

Engagement can be a very elusive term. Edward Deci provides a framework that clarifies what an employee is seeking in a job to enhance his or her feelings of self-determination. The three factors he suggests are:

1. Competence: employees want to feel competent in doing their jobs, gain mastery, and have the opportunity to develop more.
2. Connection: employees want to belong and feel attached to others.
3. Autonomy: employees want to feel in control of their behaviors and goals.

When the employee feels engaged, an important reality is that the rewards are built into the job. Instrumentality, noted above, in this case is close to 1. The employee receives the reward as a function of doing the job. The reward is intrinsic. Rewards, like recognition, are extrinsic; they may or may not occur. Pay is an extrinsic reward but has a very high instrumentality attached to it. The challenge for management is to provide a basket of rewards, both intrinsic and extrinsic, that leads to employee satisfaction.

An important discussion to have with the employee is to ask how competence, connection, and autonomy are fulfilled for the employee. The answer is frequently different from what the manager expects. Having the discussion is the essential first step.

This addresses the expectancy portion of motivation, and it can be summarized in the following formula: $(E \rightarrow P)(P \rightarrow O)(+V) =$ Motivation. Put another way, if the employee looks at the job and is confident that he or she can do it ($E \rightarrow P$, high expectancy), the firm provides outcomes that the employee finds attractive or valuable (+V), and these attractive rewards are provided ($P \rightarrow O$, high instrumentality), that employee will typically be motivated and will continue to put forth the effort needed to accomplish the task again and again. Management would conclude that the employee is a satisfied employee. All is good.

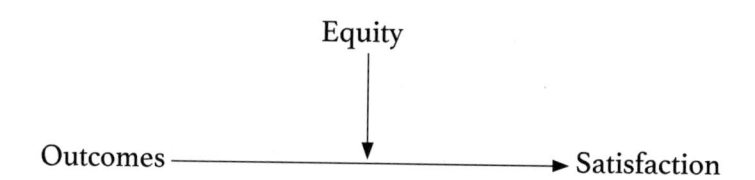

$$\begin{array}{c} \text{Equity} \\ \downarrow \\ \text{Outcomes} \longrightarrow \text{Satisfaction} \end{array}$$

The relationship between valued (+V) outcomes and satisfaction, however, is not a simple relationship. For example:

1. The employee may find out that his increase in salary at the end of the year was the same as what everyone else got. The employee may have assumed he would get more than others because he perceives himself to be a better performer, and so he is dissatisfied.
2. Management gave the employee a 2.5 percent salary increase. However, the employee was expecting a 4 percent increase. While the 2.5 percent salary increase may be competitive with the market, the employee is still dissatisfied because he or she expected more.

Adam's Equity theory recognizes that the employee is constantly comparing what he received relative to others. If the comparison suggests there is an inequity, for whatever reason, the employee will become dissatisfied. Here is the formulation for the Equity approach.

$$\frac{\text{Outcomes}}{\text{Inputs}} = \frac{\text{Outcomes}}{\text{Inputs}}$$

If the ratio of inputs and outcomes is the same, then there is equity in the relationship. Keep in mind, the employee is not looking at the salary in any absolute sense; he or she is looking at compensation relative to others. If the input of the parties is perceived as equal and the outcomes received are equal, there is equity in the relationship. All is good. Several other possibilities exist, however. Suppose both parties are not working very hard, but they are getting comparable high outcomes. The formula looks like this:

$$\frac{\text{High}}{\text{Low}} = \frac{\text{High}}{\text{Low}}$$

Both parties are satisfied because the ratio is the same and equity exists. The organization may be getting the short end of the stick, but the employees are laughing their way to the bank.

$$\frac{\text{Low}}{\text{High}} = \frac{\text{Low}}{\text{High}}$$

This is probably the more frequent perception. There is equity in the system (the ratio is the same), but the employees feel they are being screwed. If this perception is widely perceived, there is systemic inequity and bigger problems loom for the organization. Voluntary turnover will increase.

More interesting problems emerge when the inputs and outcomes are not equal. Predict employee A's response when the situation looks like this:

$$\frac{A}{\frac{High}{Low}} \neq \frac{B}{\frac{Low}{High}}$$

If employee A received a 6 percent increase in pay and the grapevine reports that employee B received a 2 percent increase, what would employee A do?

1. Feel guilty about the situation, go to his boss, request a lower increase, and ask that the remainder be given to employee B?
2. Keep the salary increase and shut up?

The equity approach says that the employee rarely, if ever, gives up positively valent outcomes, so the answer is #2. The guilt that employee A feels can be reduced by working harder and employee B, if he perceives the same situation, will typically reduce his input moving forward.

To this point, the discussion is focused on pay. The equity approach covers all positively valent outcomes, so all can be considered in the determination of equity or inequity: windows in the office, a rug on the floor or tile, a fancy phone with two lines rather than one, a designated parking space or not, and so on and so on.

If there is satisfaction in the system, this loops back and affects effort moving forward.

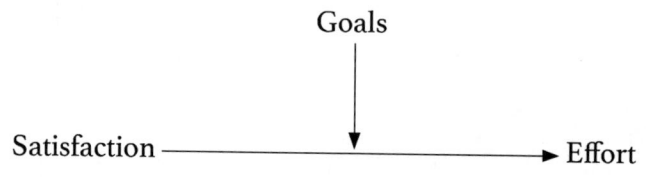

```
              Goals
                │
                ▼
Satisfaction ─────────────▶ Effort
```

The discussion to this point recognizes motivation based on rewards. The employee works to meet certain objectives (rewards), and, if they are provided when acceptable performance is achieved, the system is working effectively.

Another factor that is important in the context of motivation is goal-setting. Many parents who have raised their children but have not completed a college degree themselves. They decide that it is the time in their life when earning a college degree would be a laudable goal.

Lots of things have changed on the college campus, and the greatest determinant of the level of change is technology. The amount of technology that the parent encounters begins at the library. The parent steps into the library and seeks out the card catalog. She quickly discovers that the card catalog she knew no longer exists. She has not written a term paper in twenty-five years. Everyone has a cell phone, and few individuals talk to each other. They are focused on their cell phones. Colleagues are now twenty years younger. This is just the beginning. The assertion here is that the typical rewards of college life are a thing of the past. What drives this individual is the fact that she has set a goal (graduation), and she will endure the college experience in pursuit of that goal. It is, therefore, argued that a goal you pursue can influence positive behavior, just as returning parents will experience lots of changes and grin and bear them in the pursuit of their graduation.

The various characteristics of effective goals will facilitate accomplishing the ultimate goal. Clarity, challenge, commitment, feedback, task complexity, and self-efficiency all aid in goal accomplishment, and some of these can be addressed by management. You can discuss with employees their goals, and you might also learn what motivates them. You can then consider how these rewards might be added to the reward system. Keep in mind:

1. Motivation is a complex phenomenon, and there is no one best way to motivate an employee.
2. What people are trying to accomplish by working is open to many answers.

3. Talking with individual employees and employee groups on a continual basis is essential.
4. Job enrichment (increased tasks and/or responsibilities) will do much to improve job engagement and satisfaction.

AN INTEGRATED EXPETANCY, EQUITY AND GOAL SETTING APPROACH.

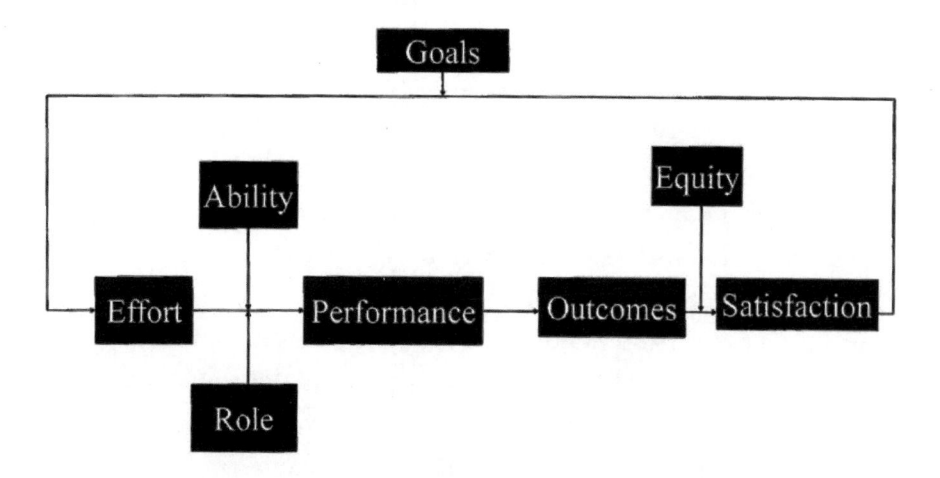

```
                    ┌─────────┐
                    │  Goals  │
                    └────┬────┘
    ┌────────────────────┼──────────────────────────────┐
    │        ┌─────────┐ │              ┌────────┐      │
    │        │ Ability │ │              │ Equity │      │
    │        └────┬────┘ │              └───┬────┘      │
    │ ┌────────┐  │  ┌───▼────────┐  ┌──────▼───┐ ┌──────────────┐
    └─│ Effort ├──┼─▶│ Performance├─▶│ Outcomes ├▶│ Satisfaction │─┘
      └────────┘  │  └────────────┘  └──────────┘ └──────────────┘
                  │
              ┌───▼──┐
              │ Role │
              └──────┘
```

Do not let the model scare you. All the pieces have been discussed above. Keep in mind that motivation is a very complex and looped affair.

Culture

Corporate culture eats strategic planning for lunch. Let me repeat that: corporate culture eats strategic planning for lunch! Culture was not mentioned in the chapter on strategy formation because it requires an entirely different mindset and a longer timeframe to appreciate and possibly change the culture. Keep this observation in mind. Culture questions and answers start on day one.

It is also typically asserted that you need a strategy before you develop a structure. When the organization consists of two entrepreneurs working out of the proverbial garage or college dorm room, the development of an organizational structure is far from anyone's mind. If the idea comes to fruition, a good lawyer and a finance person are important to cover the initial critical questions. If the plan is not to sell out but to build and grow the business, then talent acquisition becomes relevant, and so on down the line until all critical functions are covered.

At its most basic, structure is how the organizational members divide up the work. Specialization increases productivity, so how does the organization cluster people and functions?

Historically, the basic structure was functional. The organization had a marketing group, a finance group, an accounting group, a production group, and a personnel group. The names have changed, so the firm that still employs a functional design would have a marketing group, a finance group, a supply chain management group, an accounting group, and a human resources group, plus an array of additional functions as it grows. What remains the same is that the employees are grouped in homogeneous groups by function. While greater efficiencies are gained in this structure (within groups), the organization becomes less efficient when the work calls for greater collaboration *across* groups.

When collaboration becomes more important and the customer is demanding more seamless interaction with the organization, the firm assumes a product structure. In this instance, all the relevant functions that come into contact with the customer are clustered under one roof and report to a product manager or general manager. The downside of this structure is that many functions are duplicated across product groups leading to greater inefficiency. Gaining the advantages of both these structures is what the matrix structure attempts to accomplish. Functional experts are now shared across the product groups, but the evaluation of individual performance becomes more problematic, and coordination can become a deep rabbit hole.

There are certainly more structures that might be employed, but these three (function, product, matrix) provide a general lay of the land. In the section on strategy, the concept of partnership was mentioned. Given the dynamic marketplace today and the rate of change an organization's senior management encounters, the advantages of a partnership become more apparent. Mergers require both organizations to give up too much, and the success rate of mergers and acquisitions is less than impressive. Seventy percent of mergers typically fail. Lack of clear purpose, clashing business strategies and emerging conflict as the two cultures are brought together are frequent causes.

As the structure of the organization develops, the organization also develops a culture. Culture might be described by those within it as "the way we do things here and the values that we believe in." As time goes on, the culture becomes more stable and increasingly difficult to change. Some estimate that it will take seven to ten years to change the culture of an organization.

Confounding the problems associated with choosing the correct structure, there is also the "feel" that employees experience within each structure. Characterizing the rubric of feel is nicely illustrated in the work of Lee Bolman and Terrance Deal in their book *Reframing Organizations: Artistry, Choice, and Leadership*. They identify and discuss four frames that characterize the feel of organizations. The first frame is the structural frame. In this frame, the organization exists to achieve established goals, rationality prevails, appropriate forms of coordination ensure that units work together, and, when problems arise, remedies are found in restructuring. As the organization grows, more standardization and more bureaucracy seep in. Try to get through the Department of Motor Vehicles office in your state on the first try. There is always some form or letter that the customer does not have readily available.

If you would like a musical touchstone for this frame, turn to Spotify and call up Pink Floyd's song, "Another Brick in the Wall." The bigger the firm and the longer it has been nestled in its niche, the more employees feel like a number and merely another brick in the wall.

The second frame that Bolman and Deal consider is the human resource frame. In this instance, the employees and the organizations need each other. The organization needs talent, and the employees need careers, salaries, and opportunities. When imbalance emerges, one side will exploit the other. Much of the human relations movement within the history of management thought finds a close parallel with this frame, and much of the themes of participative management and employee engagement find a supportive home in this frame. Turn to Spotify again and call up the classic song by Sister Sledge, "We Are Family."

The third frame is the political frame. There is a major shift in the focus within this frame. There are various interest groups with enduring differences across these groups, most important decisions involve the allocation of scarce resources, and conflict plays a dominant role in organizational dynamics. Power emerges in bargaining, jockeying, and negotiation situations. This is not a pleasant situation in which to find yourself for most employees. Employees must continually watch their backs. The sands are continually shifting under their feet. The musical reference here is found in the Guns N' Roses song, "Welcome to the Jungle." This frame is not for the faint of heart and is 180 degrees from the human relations frame. The continual tension operative here will increase employee stress and turnover and typically result in organizational dysfunction.

The final frame is the symbolic frame. It recognizes the ambiguity employees feel and offers symbols, rituals, and ceremonies to provide the glue to hold the organization and its employees together. The musical experience for this frame is found in the Olympic National Anthem. It is very difficult to not feel the positive emotion as this song is played or sung. The relevance for a given organization is that the culture of the organization and its values provide the glue to hold the organization together and diminish the negative aspects of organizational life operative with the power struggles at play in the political frame.

The strategy chapter focused primarily on the tasks that need to be achieved for organizational sustainability. On the other side of that coin are the closely held values the organization aspires to that are absolutely necessary for long-term organizational effectiveness. How employees, and especially senior management, execute the values of the organization will determine whether the organization is dominated by the symbolic or political frame. It is very easy to slide back into the political frame and very difficult to dig out. Reform typically involves the advent of a new senior management team and then a number of years before employees learn to trust the new management team.

Another takeaway from this discussion is to recognize that the firm does not adopt just one of these frames. It is more typical that all four frames are operating at any point in time. Circumstances will dictate the relative priority of a given frame for a given circumstance. It is important to recognize which frame has most play at a given point in time and to act accordingly. Be a keen observer of what people say and then what they do. Actions speak louder than words.

In summary, the organization adopts a structure to accomplish the strategy. The organization also develops a culture as it develops its structure. The culture of the organization is very difficult to change as it weaves its way into the organizational structure.

Change Management

Organizational life is not linear, it is looped.
—Peter Senge, *The Fifth Discipline*

A Case Study

I have always believed that writing is a critical skill if you expect to be successful in your career. Given that belief, I have always had a significant writing sample as a major portion of the grade in my classes. The term paper may be 40 percent of the grade. It was week eleven of the fourteen-week semester course in organizational behavior and management. I decided to give the students a real taste of the problems associated with organizational change before launching into the lecture on that topic.

I began the lecture by saying that the Dean had convened a committee to overhaul the curriculum and that he had invited six chief executive officers from local St. Louis firms to meet and discuss the matter on a Saturday morning. Faculty who wished to come were more than welcome to attend. I reported to the class that the CEOs were very strong in their opinion that writing skills were no longer important for success on the job and that what would be more needed is to have very good interpersonal and communication skills. I told them that if the situation called for change, I was ready to do so. Therefore, I said to the class of fifty-five students that the term paper for the class was no longer required.

As a side bar, I should note that students are very territorial regarding where they sit. Within three class meetings, the seating arrangement is stable. I casually note the phenomenon at some appropriate time and provide the following observation to tweak the class: the gunners sit up front, the students in the middle don't care to be called on but they want to be seen and smile a lot, and the people in the back of the room are the underachievers.

When the announcement was made regarding the cancellation of the term paper, the reaction was both swift and predictable. Students in the front of the classroom (gunners) were absolutely dismayed at this change in the program. They were probably close to having a completed term paper that only required a final reading and the purchase of a nice plastic cover to put it in. Students who sat in the middle of the classroom were confused as to what was going on and remained quiet for a few minutes. The students in the back of the class (underachievers) were ecstatic. More likely than not, they had yet to start on the term paper and this news was simply manna from heaven.

After the initial shock began to sink in, the real fun began. "You can't do that!" "Well, I did." "We are going to report you to the Dean." "Be my guest. He was in the Saturday morning meeting, so I expect that he will be happy with my decision, but you ask him." The students in the back of the room were out of their seats and high-fiving each other as they recognized they had just dodged a bullet. As you might imagine, several angrier statements were put forth, but I essentially said "Do what you like. I am the faculty member in charge of this class, and I make the rules." I let the discussion, or I should say shouting match, go on for another twenty minutes as the students exhausted all remedies. My constant response was that times had changed and I wanted to be on the cutting edge, therefore I made a command decision.

After the twenty minutes passed, I said, "Welcome to the topic of organizational change. Your response to the news typifies the typical response of employees when management presents a new edict regarding how the organization will proceed." I then made it perfectly clear that this was just a case study. There was no conference on Saturday, and no chief executive officers had spoken about the value of writing skills. Most important, the paper had **not** been canceled. Now the fun really began. Welcome to the world of unintended consequences. You should have seen the expression and serious anger on the faces of the people in the back row. They were now going to the Dean to express their concern over the stress that I had created in my classroom. Gunners in the front rows retired to their original stance now that real order had been restored. I received the intended response from the students, and I can assure you the case study was never used again!

Change management ranks right up there with motivation and leadership when you start the search on Google. For the purposes of this book, the approach developed by Warner Burke and George Letwin provides a comprehensive delineation of the twelve major factors you must consider when contemplating change. The following considerations are in order:

1. The twelve factors are intended to address all the major factors to be considered when managing change.
2. The relations among the factors are indicated and all have feedback loops going both ways. For example, culture affects management practices and management practices affect organizational culture.
3. Most of the factors are internal to the organization, but the external environment is related both to mission and structure and to individual, group, and organizational performance.
4. The approach is broad enough that the change agent can consider a small process change in a department or a transformational change that will impact all factors organization-wide.
5. What is *not* specified is the relative influence between factors. All of this is left to the practicing manager to apply the model to his or her organization or department and determine the relative influence among related factors. What the model does do is provide a start to consider what may be changed as the change process is developed.

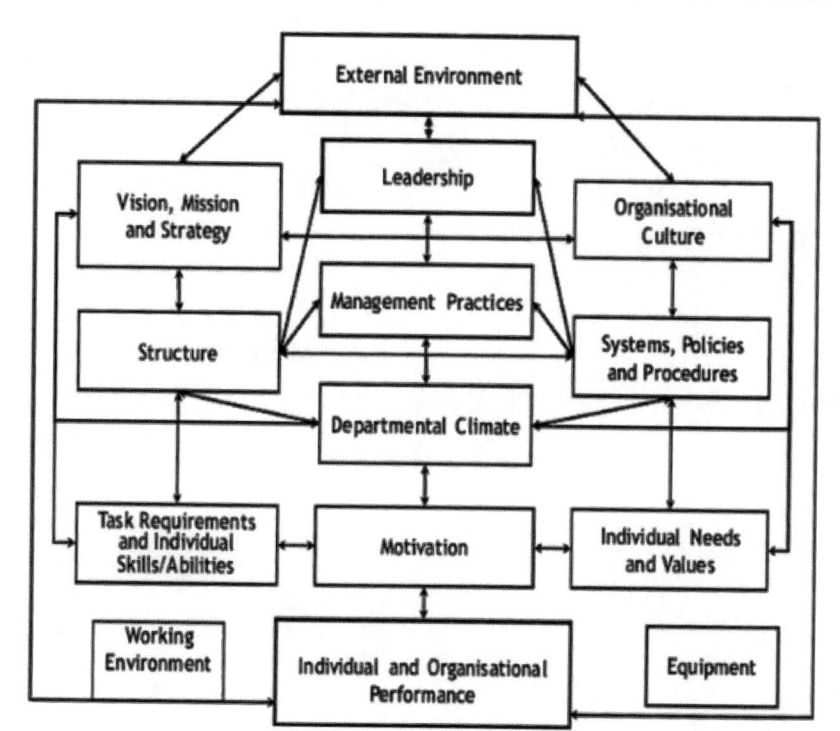

THE BURKE-LITWIN MODEL OF ORGANIZATIONAL PERFORMANCE AND CHANGE

[Diagram: Burke-Litwin Model showing interconnected boxes: External Environment at top, connected to Vision, Mission and Strategy; Leadership; and Organisational Culture. Middle layer: Structure, Management Practices, Systems, Policies and Procedures. Then Departmental Climate. Then Task Requirements and Individual Skills/Abilities, Motivation, Individual Needs and Values. Bottom: Working Environment, Individual and Organisational Performance, Equipment.]

Examples:
1. What do you think might be the relationship between the External Environment and Leadership? You might argue that a complex and dynamic environment would not support authoritarian leadership. This relationship is testable in the real world. Another individual might argue that employees are frightened by the complex environment and like an authoritarian leader to make the decisions. This is again a testable hypothesis.
2. What do you think might be the relationship between Task Requirements and Motivation? You might argue for a very positive relationship between the two. Another individual recognizes the hiring practices of the past have not prepared the current workforce for complex jobs. The result will be turmoil and more voluntary turnover.

So where does a manager start? A key assist in this regard is found in the systems thinking espoused by Peter Senge in his seminal book, *The Fifth Discipline*. The book is a challenging read, but it does demonstrate how organizations are looped rather than linear and may provide a place to start. In this regard, there are some definitions that you need to keep in mind:

1. Some loops are accelerating loops. For example, (1) the little snowball rolling down the mountainside gets bigger as it moves forward; (2) a rumor starts and quickly spreads throughout the organization; (3) a student starts to wear rain boots and pretty soon all the women are wearing rain boots; (4) a valued employee leaves the department and others in the department dust off their resumes and start looking for jobs elsewhere. These are accelerating loops.
2. Some loops are balancing loops. For example, if the temperature in the room is 72° and the resident wants the temperature to be 75°, he sets the dial at 75°. As the temperature closes in on 75°, the heater is turned down and is entirely turned off when the temperature reaches 75°. When a practicing manager comes across a dysfunctional group he or she typically intervenes but backs away as the group begins to function more effectively.
3. The third critical definition is of delays. Sometimes there is a close relationship between two factors and the impact on the second factor is noted in a fairly short period of time. In this instance, there is no delay. In another example, a firm may go through a strategic planning process and develop a well-thought-out plan. However, it may take three years before the organization sees the full implementation and impact of that strategic plan. In this instance, there is a significant delay.

Senge provides twelve generic archetypes in the glossary of his book. Three of those generic archetypes are included in the glossary of this text. They are employed to provide the expanded applications used as illustrations in this book.

There is one other discipline discussed in the book that is very relevant to the change management process. That discipline is mental models. All individuals operate with their own mental models. Here is but one for example. When the organization is on hard times and close to bankruptcy, many people begin to dust off their resumes and begin to consider other opportunities in the marketplace. That is a mental model.

Consider another possibility. For the people in the organization who are in their fifties, when they view the organization's troubles, they double down and begin to work even harder to save the organization. Their belief is that, at their age, trying to find a comparable job in the market will be very difficult. Therefore, they work diligently to maintain the job that they currently have in the organization. This is, again, a mental model.

Here is a fully developed model to illustrate how this process works.

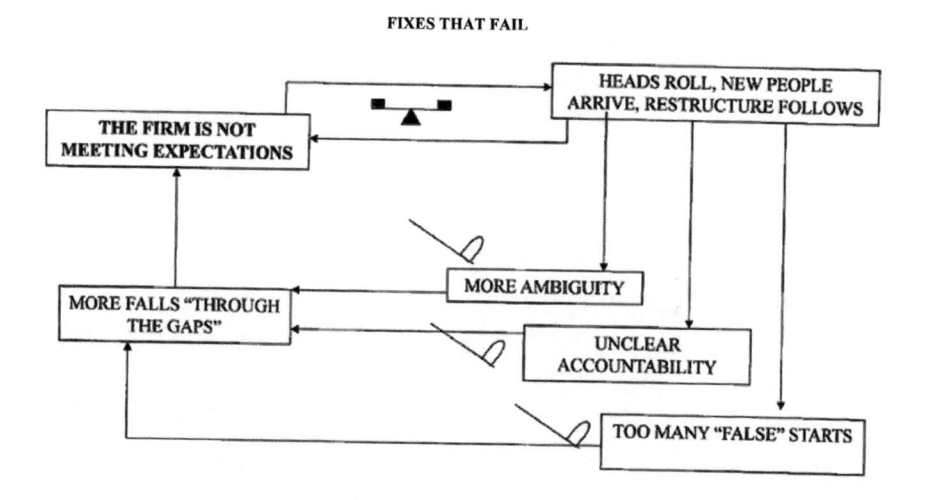

FIXES THAT FAIL

```
                              ┌──────────────────────────────────┐
                              │  HEADS ROLL, NEW PEOPLE          │
                              │  ARRIVE, RESTRUCTURE FOLLOWS     │
┌──────────────────────┐      └──────────────────────────────────┘
│ THE FIRM IS NOT      │
│ MEETING EXPECTATIONS │
└──────────────────────┘
                                    ┌──────────────────┐
                                    │ MORE AMBIGUITY   │
┌──────────────────────┐             └──────────────────┘
│ MORE FALLS "THROUGH  │             ┌──────────────────┐
│      THE GAPS"       │             │ UNCLEAR          │
└──────────────────────┘             │ ACCOUNTABILITY   │
                                     └──────────────────┘
                                     ┌────────────────────────┐
                                     │ TOO MANY "FALSE" STARTS│
                                     └────────────────────────┘
```

The mental model that explains this archetype goes like this. The board engages in hiring a new CEO. If it is an evolutionary transition, the CEO typically experiences an initial honeymoon. If the situation dictates a revolutionary change, actions to remedy the situation begin to occur immediately. Regardless of which end of the spectrum is in play, the firm's employees typically take a wait-and-see attitude as the new CEO enters the organization.

The new CEO does not lead the charge for change as a single individual. He or she has the current senior management team to assist in the transition. Some transitions within the senior management team are inevitable. The departures may be at the initiation of the senior management employees, or they may be at the discretion of the new CEO. Regardless as to why departures from the senior management team are occurring, the goal is to develop an effective senior management team ready and willing to take on the key challenges the organization faces. This process does not occur in a quick fashion. It may take up to twelve to eighteen months for the new senior management team to be in place and operating effectively. The board of directors views this entire transition as a balancing loop. The seesaw (▬▬▲▬▬) indicated a balancing loop.

The new CEO is on board, and he or she puts a new management team in place. As appropriate, strategic planning takes place, and the organization becomes more effective as time goes on. At least, this is the hope. So the question that needs to be asked is why the transition to a new CEO typically has substantial bumps in the road. To answer this question, you need to look at what is happening within the organization during this transition. With the advent of new members to the senior management team, new approaches to meeting the organization's problems emerge. These changes do not occur overnight. The results among members of the organization's employees are noted in the lower half of the archetype. Typically, what results as the new people arrive and new structures are put into place is that employees experience more ambiguity as to what is expected, unclear accountability for actions to be taken begins to emerge, and, quite possibly, too many false starts occur, particularly if small changes are made in this transition process. All three of these are accelerating loops and result in more activities falling through the gaps. The snowball ( ) rolling down the mountainside indicates an accelerating loop. These three accelerating loops create a negative impact on the organization's attempt to meet expectations. If this situation becomes severe, there will be further cries that the new CEO is ineffective and must go. The hoped-for balancing loop becomes a nightmare for the organization.

You might ask: just how long does change at this level of the organization take to bear fruit? For illustration, assume that one of the major activities of the new CEO and his or her management team is to change the organizational culture. It is argued here that changing the culture of an organization will probably take seven to ten years. In the face of this transition is the fact that the tenure of chief executive officers typically resides in the three-to-five-year range. This further leads to the churning phenomenon that is operative at this level of organizational change.

Two additional factors complicate the change process. The first is the amount of change that decision-makers think is necessary to accomplish the desired outcome. In many instances, the interventions are grossly inadequate. As an example, consider the Exxon Valdez situation. The captain of the ship recognized that he was on course to run aground and decided to immediately stop the engines and put them into full reverse. Knowledgeable people have noted that the ship would continue in its original path for at least three further miles before the boat would stop and begin to reverse direction. You might argue that a more effective intervention would have been to change the direction of the ship's rudder. True enough. Suffice to say, the initial remedy was not enough. The lesson here is to carefully examine the parameters of the situation and introduce an equally sufficient array of remedies to effectively solve the problem.

The second factor addresses the quality of the information that decision-makers employ to address a problem. In this day of fake news, you are hard-pressed to have confidence in the quality of the information employed to resolve problems.

As mentioned, one of the essential disciplines that Peter Senge addresses is mental models. The observations provided above to illustrate the archetype are mental models. Those mental models belong to this author. Other HR professionals may assert their own mental models. The development of mental models that both are accurate (explain what is going on) and provide reasonable solutions employs both art and science. The development of mental models also leans heavily upon the experience base of all HR professionals with an experienced level of wisdom concerning these issues. This point cannot be overemphasized. All employees have mental models. The test of the mental model is in these questions: does it accurately explain what is transpiring within the firm, and does it provide useful approaches for resolving the issues affecting the organization?

In summary, Peter Senge provides twelve archetypes which can be found in the back of his book. They are very good pump primers for anyone wishing to clarify their own mental models in a more rigorous and formal fashion. It takes practice but is well worth the effort. A useful exercise would be to have the members of the management team propose their mental models and then discuss them among the group. Over time, a group will develop its own mental models. The outcome may be a collection of group meta-models relating to how the organization works.

Integrating the Burke model and Senge's Systems Thinking is a tough challenge, but the payoffs can be substantial. To put it succinctly, the Burke model provides the what of change, while Senge's archetypes provide the process of change, and our mental models provide the grease for change activities.

In Practice

The work of Burke and Senge will be revisited in the second section of the book, and its implications for change will be explored further then. The work of Peter Senge is important when developing your view about how change works. At the strategic level, there are some important considerations and recommendations to keep in mind.

1. Communication, communication, communication: it cannot be stressed enough.
2. Receiving input from those affected by the change is critical.
3. Build the change process so that there are successes along the way. Make sure to celebrate the successes. It provides the opportunity to reaffirm where the organization is going.
4. Assess the need for resources to accomplish the next phase. Have changes occurred that dictate a change in plans? These in-process reviews are critical to ultimate success.

Introduction to the HRM Section

The senior management members of firms are quick to point out the importance of human resources to the long-term sustainability of their organization. This has become increasingly evident in the face of addressing COVID-19 and its impact on the supply of individuals willing to work for the organization. It has turned into a double whammy.

There is less of a supply of available talent due to the COVID virus. Moreover, there are many employees who are now questioning how they wish to pursue their careers. Do they want a full-time job? Many people are now desiring to work from home or pursue other arrangements that are different from the traditional full-time position based in the organization's office.

These considerations are placing substantial burdens on the human resource departments of today's organizations. Where are the workers supposed to come from, and what are the demands that they will place on the organization for their continued participation? The mission statements of many of the top corporations amply note the value of human resources to the organization. These new wrinkles, however, are yet to be addressed in a meaningful fashion in these mission statements.

The supply of valued employees is not the only major factor to consider in today's business environment. A sampling of major factors affecting organizations in the year 2022 is listed below. While all are important, all do not have the same priority for the human resources department. HR departments cannot afford to attempt to boil the ocean. Some of these factors are beyond the scope of the organization to affect in any meaningful fashion. What the effective HR department needs to do is to come up with some meaningful categorization scheme that will assist in making the list more manageable and assigning responsibility for addressing it.

Here is one proposed categorizations scheme:
- Factors that are very important but are beyond the capacity of the organization to resolve. It may contribute to a resolution but will not be the major force of resolving the issue.
- Factors that are relevant to the organization and the organization has the capability of addressing the factor, but it will require the support of all. It is an all hands on deck type of issue.
- Factors that are relevant to the organization and can be addressed by the HR department.

What becomes evident very quickly is that there are very few factors that fall in the third category. The HR department may be assigned responsibility to address the given factor, but the success of steps taken to address the factor inevitably require support from the larger organization.

Our conclusion is that this is not the most effective approach for determining the roles and activities of the HR department. The list still remains relevant to the organization and its employees because, in the aggregate, it provides a global list of factors that, if addressed and resolved, contribute to the long-term sustainability of the organization.

Therefore, the recommendation is to review the list annually, to ask how the organization is responding to five of the macro issues, and to also pick five of the more micro issues that the organization is addressing and set achievable annual goals that move the organization forward in addressing these issues.

Major Factors in 2022

Keep in mind the important observation of Thomas Sowell: "There are no solutions, only trade-offs."

Artificial Intelligence
Diversity
The Gig Economy
Cloud-Based HR Technology
Change Management: Agile Adaptation and Smooth Changes
Leadership
People Management Skills: Empathy, Providing Resources, Mediation
Diversity and Inclusion
The Great Resignation and Global Ramifications
Workforce Optimization and Automation to Address Labor Shortage
The Skills Gap with Value-Driven Metrics
Understanding Younger Workers
New Ways to Engage Employees
Employee Wellness Is a Priority
Modern Benefits to Boost Retention
More Data-Driven HR
Block Chain Improves Security
Deeper Role in Corporate Strategy
Focus on Reskilling Workers
Increased Investment in Leadership Development
Growing Opportunities for ONA
HR Chatbots Become the Norm
Text Message Recruiting Is on the Rise
Focusing on Internal Talent Mobility
Moving Toward Continuous Performance Management

Again, keep in mind the important observation of Thomas Sowell: "There are no solutions, only trade-offs."

Put another way, optimization is the efficient and reasonable allocation of limited resources against the challenges the organization faces.

Scope of the Work for HR

The Society for Human Resource Management's (SHRM) learning program provides a good indication of what the professional field thinks is important. These activities are strategy formation, manpower management, human resource development, compensation, employment and labor law, and risk analysis. All these content areas are necessary in an effective HR response to people issues in the organization.

Another possible framework for HR activities is to develop an agenda around the following: attraction, selection, performance management, manpower development, career development, and retention activities for valued employees. Each of these activities can be considered individually, but it is more fruitful to consider these collectively as part of an accelerating loop that is the foundation of human resource management.

Stated simply, if the organization hires good people, these people will be effective in their positions. Collective employee performance produces good outcomes that lead to effective organizational performance and long-term organizational stability. As the organization develops, it invests in the development of its employees and provides career advancement opportunities. In the longer term, the organization is recognized as an employer of choice and this enhances the attraction of future valued employees. There are many accelerating loops that can be explored, but this foundational accelerating loop is the central argument of this book. We use this argument moving forward.

The Selection Process

The job interview is often perceived as the critical assessment tool for evaluating a candidate's capacity and competence for a job. Companies make decisions based on the initial (and sometimes singular) interview or a series of interviews, and job seekers do as well. The selection interview is known as a very poor predictor of future job performance, but it is still the most frequently utilized tool in the selection process. If it continues to be the instrument of choice, what can be done to improve it?

It's really a two-way street and should be managed by the organization as such. A google search for "informational interview" yields about 89,200,000 results so this is not a one size fits all topic. But for a manager with a task and deliverables list that may seem untenable, the straightforward guidance offered here may relieve some of the pressure on both managerial time and results related to the selection process.

One statement for every hiring manager to remember is this: past performance is not the only predictor of future job performance, but it is frequently viewed as the *best* predictor of future performance. This applies to life in general, and more specifically to work-related factors such as stability, temperament, and productivity/performance. For this reason, companies often employ a behavioral-based interviewing approach that limits a candidate's ability to speak of what he or she thinks should be executed in a particular situation.

In a complementary approach, the candidate is asked to provide examples of actual behaviors previously employed and then report on the outcomes that followed. It is important to remember to ask the right questions that probe for past performance indicators. The candidate is also assessing the extent to which his behaviors fit the organizational profile of what should be done in a particular situation. What follows are some tricks of the trade questions gleaned from the vast number of available websites and articles offered for improving the selection interview process.

Many company interviews begin with a human resources representative or hiring manager asking questions such as:

- Tell me about yourself.
- What do you know about our company?
- What do you know about this position, and why is it of interest you?
- What are the skills you possess that make you qualified for the job?
- Where do you see your career taking you in five years' time?
- What are some of the situations you faced in your prior job that are related to this job, and how did you handle the most complex problems that arose?

The approach is to use nondirective questions that do not permit yes or no responses. These are very good starting questions. There are probably one or two of the questions that provide the opportunity for the interviewer to further probe the candidate's past performance, leading the questions to then become more directive. Did you consider alternative courses of action? What were they? How did you decide to execute what you did? What criteria did you employ? What was your role in the issue—i.e., did you take the lead in a solution, or just take meeting notes and distribute? If you had it to do over again, would you take the same approach? Etc.

Another complementary approach explores in-depth how the candidate initially chose a position and then why the candidate left the position.

1. How did you learn about/get your position?
2. Why did you leave?

A candidate will talk more and usually offer more about him or herself than you might expect. Adults typically love to share information about themselves and their history—and for this reason, asking those two simple questions will elicit an extemporaneous (versus rehearsed) response.

In order to execute the interview questions accurately, you must begin with the earliest position indicated on a resume or application and work toward the current or most recent position. Sounds too easy, right? Actually, these two questions can be deemed the most telling of individual past performance.

For example, consider candidate Brian who has arrived for an in-person interview with you. It's a 1:1, and you are the hiring manager and will make a go/no-go recommendation. Brian has over ten years in your business arena, but he has changed companies and positions four times in those ten years. Depending on the industry and geography, that may be a normal, acceptable work history, as switching companies to obtain new challenges, higher titles and scope, and more money is not unusual in certain sectors.

But in this case, Brian has stayed in the same city and his resume does not indicate that he made job changes for title expansion and responsibility. So here is the mock interview:

Q: How did you learn about/get your position?
Brian: *Well, I had just graduated college and had interned at the company in my senior year, and they made an offer to hire me after graduation.*
Q: Why did you leave?
Brian: *So after about nine months I realized that I was not doing the work I thought I was going to be doing. My degree is in international business, and I was essentially making documents and files for senior management to use with clients. I wanted a new challenge.*

OK, let's try the next job in chronological order:

Q: How did you learn about/get your position?
Brian: *My colleagues started leaving my prior employer to work for a competitor, and they contacted me as they knew I was ready to make a move and encouraged me to apply. It wasn't much more money, but I was going to have more responsibilities and maybe not have to work so late on weeknights meeting last-minute deadlines. So a better work schedule was an attractive parameter.*
Q: Why did you leave?
Brian: *It was a pretty good job, but I felt that I wasn't being utilized to my full capacity, and I started looking on the Web to see who was hiring.*

Sounds reasonable, right? These first two positions were in Brian's early career and not meeting his personal expectations. But there's a past performance clue in his response: working late on weeknights and meeting deadlines were two aspects of the positions that were undesirable. Depending on the nature of the current business, urgency and tight deadlines may be required.

Q: How did you learn about the next position?
Brian: *There were many openings on the Web, and I applied to XYZ company, and they seemed excited to interview me. I knew that my skills were in demand, and I was hired, and I gave two weeks' notice and left.*
Q: Why did you leave?
Brian: *I mean, it's not something I planned to do initially, but my manager was not giving me enough credit for the work I was doing, so I'm glad I left. I just felt sort of unappreciated.*

Sounds reasonable again. Most employees enjoy a supportive and positive work environment. But maybe Brian's work performance was not positive and deserving of praise. It might be that the boss simply does not coach and provide feedback regularly. As the interviewer, you would not know details unless more directive questions followed. You could probe further, but it is still a past performance indicator of Brian's tolerance, temperament, and stability.

Is Brian a candidate for your organization in that he looks like he would be a good fit based on his past performance, skills, and experience? And conversely, how do you look to Brian? As much as Brian needs to convey his aptitude and capacity for the job opening, you also want to provide honest responses about the organization's culture, expectations, growth goals, etc. Brian should be interviewing you as much as you are him.

Interviews often conclude with the hiring manager asking a final question: "Do you have any questions for me?" That is a closed question and will often lead to two responses:

1. "No" or
2. "What is the next step, when do you expect to fill the position, and how soon will I hear back?"

Instead, a more open-ended, dialogue-based approach could be employed:

1. "What have you heard today that you find intriguing?"
2. "How would you rate this position in comparison to others that you are looking at?"
3. "What do you find of concern about the position?"

If you assume that the typical job interview lasts about thirty minutes, it is easy to see how the time can be quickly consumed. The confusion in the job interview is not caused simply by the amount of time given to it. As a matter of a fact, more time may simply lead to more unanswered questions.

As the interview is a two-way street, an alternative view is to consider the goals that the candidate and the interviewer each bring to the conversation. Two goals dominate:

1. Both parties want to look good to the other. The candidate wants to separate him- or herself from all the other candidates being considered for the position. At the same time, the interviewer wants to portray the organization as an employer of choice with interesting work and assignments and an attractive benefits package. Answers to questions may be shaded to put the candidate and employer into attractive lights.
2. On the other hand, both parties wish to gain information. The candidate wants to gain as much information as possible about the organization. What is the climate/culture of the organization? Is the organization more hierarchical or egalitarian? What are the advancement opportunities? Etc. In answer to these questions, the candidate is looking for direct and candid responses. The more the candidate pursues issues with directive questions, the more the possibility that he is viewed as less attractive. The organization suffers the same fate. If the questions are direct and probing, the candidate may view the organization as less attractive. Needless to say, the interview is loaded with opportunities for conflict. No wonder it is a poor predictor of future job performance.

The diagram below illustrates the two-way relationship between the candidate and the interviewer. Assuming both want to look good and gain the necessary information, it is important to pay attention to comments and questions that may cause conflict and disrupt the flow of information. If either asks or describes a conflicting message, the interview may be considered over at that point. Such conflicting information may be delivered by either party and hidden in even a single word within a sentence. For example, if the hiring manager states, "We are *aggressively* growing," the candidate may interpret it as either long hours and potentially weekends (individual circumstance will drive the conflict) or opportunities for personal impact and promotion/advancement. Honesty wins here. If the candidate has personal issues that require a hard stop at 5:00 p.m., then aggressive growth is not looking good, and the interview may be over with that single word. Or, if the candidate has only a 5:30 a.m. gym schedule and has a high need for achievement, then maybe the organization is looking good, and that message presents no conflict. Pay attention to conflicting information, as it may be a red flag and another indicator that past performance is the best predictor of future performance.

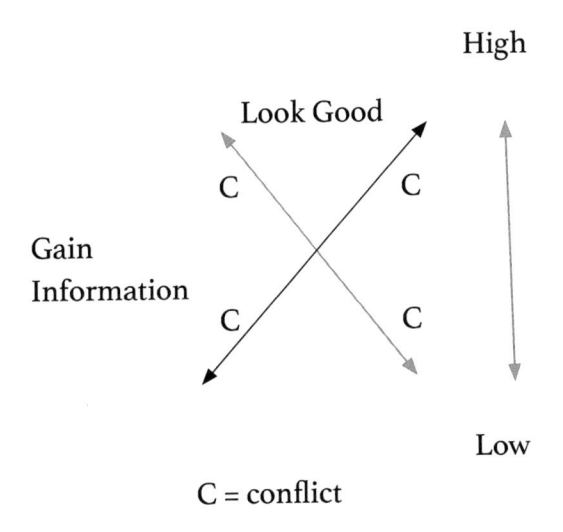

High

Look Good

C   C

Gain Information

C   C

Low

C = conflict

The second diagram (with its hourglass shape) indicates that there is a myriad of factors that may be in the mix between the candidate and the interviewer in this day and age due to the fact that all employers are seeking valued candidates. To show how confounding this may be, in the 1990s there was a shortage of nurses. The operative and sole test for hiring a nurse was "Can she fog a mirror?" If he/she is breathing, hire him/her. At the base of the hourglass, you find the outcomes (job performance leading to desired outcomes). In many instances, these are difficult to measure, and they change quickly in the ever-changing environment organizations face today.

Between all the factors that might fill the top half of the hourglass (performance inputs) and the bottom of the hourglass (performance outcomes) sits the thirty-minute interview. Little ground can be accurately covered in this short period of time. Therefore, limiting questions to those that elicit the most telling performance examples is crucial. Additionally, since a candidate pool can fluctuate and the demand for specialized skills can change (as in the nurse example), it is even more critical to leverage your abilities as an interviewer. Drill down using the simple questions provided here, redirect as needed, especially if a conflict arises between your expectations and the candidate's responses, and essentially allow them to talk.

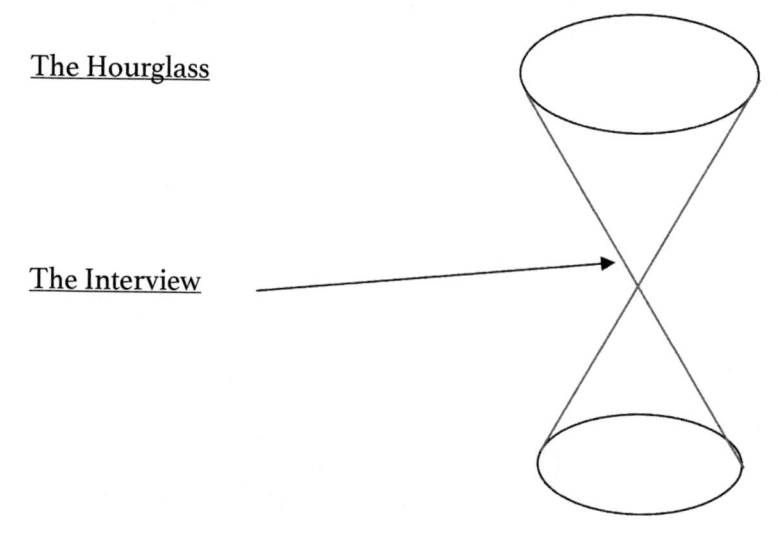

The Hourglass

The Interview

Additional sources of information need to be incorporated into the selection process.

1. Checking references is a good place to start. Do these after the interview because the interviewer will then have a foundation from which to ask probing and leading questions.
2. Assessment tests can be employed to make sure the candidate has the needed skills to perform the job functions. *Disclaimer: the author suggests consulting with legal counsel as testing/assessments must be related only to job content.*
3. Finally, the individual can be hired and then perform on the job within a specified period on a contract basis. If it is eventually decided the individual cannot execute the job, dismissal is easy.

Compensation

The topic of compensation holds a special place in the discourse of human resources management for two reasons. The first is that compensation, for the majority of employees, is the means by which employees generate resources to address many of the employee's essential needs. Meeting the food and shelter requirements for a family, paying the health care bills that arise over time, and educating the children are some of the most basic that come to mind. What is the first thing that comes to mind when you hear the word Compensation? Income? Money? Paycheck? As managers it is important to remember that compensation is more than just a paycheck. It is the means by which most of the other needs are met. This section will focus on Total Rewards, what you need to know about the legal environment and how to administer pay in a fair, consistent manner. The second reason that compensation takes such a prominent place in human resource management is the fact that it is much easier to measure than many of the other outcomes associated with human resources development (HRD).

Total Rewards is a term used to describe the intrinsic and extrinsic aspects of a well-rounded compensation program. Begin by understanding what motivates employees, in addition to base pay. Frameworks such as Maslow's Hierarchy of Needs and Herzberg's Two Factor Theory provide some interesting lists. Lots of others, however, are worthy of consideration: the employee might consider the actual work environment, organizational culture, leadership values, degree of stress, flexibility, clear expectations, and array of benefits offered. Management might also focus on learning some of the employee's wants and development opportunities, learning experiences, performance management, succession planning and training. There are other rewards that go a long way to creating a satisfied employee. Do not underestimate the power of recognition, whether it be a formalized program such as variable pay, bonus, stock options, or that of more a personal nature. A word of "thanks," "great job," or "way to go" can go a long way.

Work-life balance is another area that has been getting a lot of attention recently. When the COVID-19 pandemic forced employees to work from home, many found the work-life balance that they had been needing and requesting for a long time. Employers who do not accommodate flexibility in their organization's philosophy might risk the opportunity of being part of "The Great Resignation." Benefits must be competitive and varied to meet the needs of a multi-generational workforce. Successful organizations are committed to providing a highly competitive and comprehensive total compensation package for their employees.

Because compensation has played such a critical role in meeting employees' essential needs, there are a number of state and federal laws regulating compensation practices. It is imperative that those who maintain the compensation system study and at least be familiar with the legislation to some degree. Remember, when state and federal laws conflict, always defer to the law most advantageous to the employee. As a best practice, know where to get the most current information in the event that an issue needs to be referred to the organization's legal team (https://www.dol.gov/general/aboutdol is a great place to start). Below is a listing of the legislation and regulations that might arise:

Davis-Bacon Act
Securities Exchange Act
Walsh-Healey Public Contracts Act
Fair Labor Standards Act of 1938 (FLSA)
The Equal Pay Act
Title VII of the Civil Rights Act of 1964
Age Discrimination in Employment Act (ADEA)

Pregnancy Discrimination Act (PDA)
Americans with Disabilities Act (ADA)
Civil Rights Act of 1991
Family and Medical Leave Act (FMLA)
Mental Health Act
Worker Economic Opportunity Act
Sarbanes-Oxley Act
Securities and Exchange Commission rule change on executive compensation disclosure (SEC)
Lilly Ledbetter Fair Pay Act
Troubled Asset Relief Program (TARP)
American Recovery and Reinvestment Act of 2009 (ARRA)
Dodd-Frank Wall Street Reform and Consumer Protection Act
Wages and Fair Labor Standards Act
Worker Adjustment and Retraining Notification Act (WARN)
Immigration and Nationality Act
Uniformed Services Employment and Reemployment Rights Act (USERRA)
National Labor Relations Act (NLRA)

The members of the HR department are not expected to be practicing attorneys, but having a basic understanding of what led to the regulation, what the law is attempting to remedy, and how to establish practices to minimize problems represent sound practices.

In addition to knowing the laws noted above, it is best practice to understand basic concepts related to overtime, exemptions and hours of work, the living wage, determining who is an employee versus an independent contractor, prevailing wage issues, antitrust issues, pay discrimination, reverse discrimination, disparate treatment, and disparate impact.

The purpose of the compensation program is to provide programs and administer services in a compliant, fair, and consistent manner.

This is accomplished by comprehensive plan design and administration, along with effective communication and manager education. The ultimate goal is to maintain overall salaries that are competitive with the external market and are internally equitable. Most organizations attempt to accomplish this goal by using a market-based job evaluation philosophy. It has been said that compensation is more of an art than a science. In many instances, a seasoned practitioner has learned to understand the market data and how it will fit into the current structure of the department, division, and organization in its totality.

Based on standard practices and a systematic approach, market pricing is data-driven and defensible if challenged. Targeting the market median based on data from salary surveys representing similar organizations with comparable scopes is the most widely used pay practice. Once a median or midpoint has been determined, calculating a range of pay is completed to establish minimum and maximum data points for each range. A typical range may include all jobs with survey salaries between 80 percent and 120 percent of the midpoint.

Market pricing is the act of evaluating each job against local, state, or national survey data. In some instances, a match is found between an employer's job and a position referenced in the data, based on core duties and responsibilities of the role. This job is typically referred to as a benchmark job.

Survey data is available to participate in and purchase through numerous third-party consulting firms. It is important to match positions against key responsibilities based on job descriptions, not by matching titles. Aside from base pay, information requested and provided in the survey will include total compensation (base plus bonus plus long-term incentives), the size of the organization, number of employees represented by the data, industry, and location. Market data is available in almost every industry and discipline. It is best practice to find matches from at least three different survey sources. If no match to the job is available in survey data, the role is slotted to match the market median of jobs with similar value to the organization. Once determined, the associated minimum and maximum is applied. In every event, the final step in the evaluation process is to consider internal equity.

Before making an offer to an internal or external candidate, review criteria such as the education and experience of incumbents currently in the role, qualifications, performance, time in role, and base pay. Remember, some have said that compensation is more of an art than a science.

Careful review of internal equity is the key to avoiding litigation. Compensation policies must be compliant, consistent, and easily understood. Exceptions to policy will need to be granted occasionally but should not be the norm. Documentation as to the reason for the exception, who requested it, and who granted the exception must be kept on file in the event of a Department of Labor investigation. Not only is consistency necessary for legal reasons, but it also gives the employee a sense of trust in the process. New managers quickly learn that it is much easier to defend a decision made when the rules have not been bent or broken. Playing favorites or consistently recognizing the same employee can lower morale and create dissension within the most amiable of teams.

Knowing that employees have a right to discuss wages and that policies that specifically prohibit the discussion of wages are unlawful may be enough of a motivator to value compliance and consistency. More than that, it is the right thing to do.

Compensation is personal, linked to self-worth and identity. Take the time to get to know each member of the team and what motivates them on a personal level. Reward them in a way that they will appreciate and value.

Two Current Challenges

The advent of COVID-19 coupled with the arrival of the millennial generation has created additional challenges to the HR department and deserves some special attention. The generational categories are typically clustered into four groupings. They are:

Millennials (born 1981–2000)
Generation X (1965–1981)
Baby Boomers (1946–1965)
Traditionalists (1900–1946)

These classifications may vary depending upon the site referenced, but you do not need to parse the details to gain from the insight. Consider the millennials. Some may just be graduating from college, but some are in their early thirties, and, most importantly, they represent the largest generation in the US workforce. Control over their schedules, striking a balance between work and leisure, working remotely, and participating in rapid professional development are some of the key employment attributes for this group.

The advent of COVID-19 propelled the movement toward working from home, much to the joy of the millennials. The result is that the work still got done, so now these employees want to continue the arrangement and are pushing to secure this approach to work for the future. This situation is complemented by the advances in internet connectivity, and these will only continue in terms of the speed and sophistication of the technology available today. The paths for the future regarding how work will be conducted are under significant flux. The HR department will need to stay on top of the changes and, in many instances, will need to adapt if it wishes to attract and secure this generational cohort.

The second significant change is that we are living longer. Retirement funds may not last for the expected life timetable. Some may reenter the workforce to meet these financial shortfalls. Others may decide that staying home is not all that it was cracked up to be, so these individuals may reenter the workforce also. They have the experience needed by many employers today. At the same time, they will no longer be as compliant as they were in the past. This makes for an employee cohort that may be difficult to manage.

The bottom line for the HR department is that managing the workforce of the twenty-first century brings unique challenges that will test the capabilities of the HR department and senior management to harness these employee skills and concerns. Compensation practices remain a significant tool for attracting and engaging the workforce. However, additional perks and work arrangements will play an important role going forward.

Performance Management

The biggest problem surrounding this significant management responsibility is when the direct manager lets marginal or poor performance slide. There is the hope that the problem will self-correct. If no improvement is noted, this is typically the dominant issue discussed when the employee's annual performance review is scheduled. The annual review is then the last occasion where the poor performance is addressed.

In the first situation, the manager dreads the day the meeting is to occur. The advice given to the manager is to use the Oreo approach: start with some good news at the beginning of the review, then hit the employee with the bad news in the middle of the review, and then conclude the meeting with some more pro forma good news. It sounds good, but it rarely carries the day. If the employee is expecting a poor review, he is preparing all plausible excuses for the poor performance. Armed with this information, he responds aggressively to the information the boss puts on the table. The boss is looking for compliance and a promise to do better. What is not expected is an assertive argument for all the obstacles standing in the way. Rest assured, all the blame rests with others and/or the circumstances surrounding the situation.

The other situation is when the employee is not expecting a bad review and is blindsided by the less than positive news. The typical reaction is, "Why didn't you tell me earlier when I could have corrected the situation?" From this point on, the situation spins into greater dysfunction. The employee dusts off the resume and engages in more dysfunctional behavior and rarely mends his ways without further constructive coaching on the part of the manager.

There must be a better way! The most effective way to address performance management is to recognize it as an ongoing process, not a one-time meeting at the end of the year. The process begins during the initial interview when the position responsibilities are discussed and carries on in earnest during the first meeting between the new employee and his or her boss. The process has the following stages:

- Setting expectations and performance goals
- Providing FAST feedback (see below)
- Discussing and promoting further skill development opportunities
- Assessing the employee's potential for advancement in a professional or managerial role
- Considering potential transfer and/or possible termination if it is determined that the organization made a bad hiring decision.

If these steps are followed consistently, many of the negative feelings associated with the annual review will disappear and many positive outcomes will follow.

As discussed earlier, the selection interview is constrained by the amount of time typically devoted to it and the fact that so many other agenda items are at play. Few things are remembered. Therefore, it is essential that the newly hired employee and the manager take the time to fully discuss what the expectations regarding job performance and the performance goals for the employee will be over a specified period of time. The discussion is a two-way street. The employee should also be given time to express his or her expectations regarding the manager's performance in support of the newly hired employee. This might also include the responsibilities of the rest of the management team and fellow employees. The goal here is to communicate to all parties a clear set of expectations and goals for all. Yes, it is a team sport.

This meeting should be the first of many. While the first meeting may be more formal and planned, additional meetings may occur as the situation develops. The manager may also appoint a more senior employee to be the initial mentor for the new employee. This is an effective way to promote good performance behaviors, and it also indicates to the employee that the organization is doing all it can to ensure a good start for the employee. The duration of this more formal introduction to the job is most likely determined by the nature of the job. If it is an entry level position, the initial mentoring program may last a week or two. If the position responsibilities are more complex, the initial mentoring period may be a matter of months.

When the formal introduction to the job is completed, issues surrounding expected behaviors still persist. When marginal behaviors are exhibited in this time frame, the intervention should follow the lead of FAST feedback proposed by Bruce Tulgan. FAST is a good acronym for what needs to occur regarding performance feedback in this instance. The intervention should be Frequent, Accurate, Specific, and Timely. The intervention should come as soon as feasible, given the occurrence of the marginal behavior, and the intervention should be accurate. Point out the specific marginal behavior and then determine what should be occurring in this instance. If these three steps are taken, the employee should be receiving accurate information concerning the appropriate behaviors.

If the FAST system is employed, there should be little need to hash these issues over in the annual review. The annual review can then focus on the developmental recommendations for the employee, given what has been observed over the last year. If the employee likes the professional nature of the work and desires to remain in the role, what are the additional training and task assignments that would benefit both the individual and organization? Assignment to a project may provide some of these opportunities to develop new skills.

It may be that the employee would like to pursue a more managerial role over time. If this is the case, the individual may be assigned the lead position on a departmental project. The employee may discover that management is not as attractive as originally thought. If this is the case, it is good to discover early on, and the employee can return to his original assignment when the project is completed. The experience may also indicate that the individual has the potential for this kind of work but that there are current deficiencies that need to be addressed. This is important information, and remedies can now be identified and implemented to meet this need. Practice makes perfect, and this approach permits practice with relatively low risk. The employee and the organization both learn and are not tasked with the job of demoting an individual who did not work out.

Keep in mind that several motivational factors are at play in this process. Advancement is, typically, a highly sought-after prize, and the organization needs individuals with advanced professional and managerial skills for long-term success. The approach suggested here provides plenty of opportunity to test an employee's skills, both professional and managerial. The important part is that these opportunities should be planned by management to ensure the organization has the manpower needed for the long term. If the employee does not see the opportunity to test his or her skills, the individual will most likely look elsewhere. In this instance, the organization is losing its most prized employees to voluntary turnover.

Advancement up the managerial hierarchy presents interesting and complex issues. There is not a defined set of skills needed to be a successful manager or leader. The first step in this process is typically as a lead person in the department. The individual is offered this management position primarily because of his technical skills. This person is there to assist in the development of the less experienced employees in the department. Having this type of individual available always reduces the amount of time it takes to get the new hires up to speed. The result is that the department is working to capacity and producing expected outcomes earlier rather than later.

Advancement to the position of manager of the department requires a qualitatively different set of skills. The manager is ultimately responsible for the performance of the department. However, if the department has qualified lead persons, the manager can devote a substantial portion of his or her time to interaction with other department managers. It is difficult to measure, but the interaction and collaboration among related departments is essential to the effectiveness of the entire enterprise. Departments are not dependent on each other, nor are they independent. They are interdependent. Striking the appropriate balance among interdependent departments is more art than science. Persuasive skills become the most important set of skills in this interaction. Listening carefully to determine the perspective of other department heads becomes imperative. A manager may develop a "Eureka!" decision that all adhere to. Often, though, the decision will be a negotiated solution, so negotiation skills become important. Sometimes, there will be no decision, and in this instance the manager needs to tell the other manager to go to hell in such a manner that he is looking forward to taking the trip. There will be another day, and you do not wish to burn bridges.

The effective middle manager will probably spend his or her entire career in middle management positions. These positions are essential to the sustainability of the organization. This is where the rubber hits the road when considering the effectiveness of the organization. History resides here. Careful decision-making that determines the firm's long-term effectiveness occurs here.

The third level of management is labeled senior management. This level of the organization is devoted to identifying and developing the long-term strategy for the organization. Mergers are considered and resolved at this level. Buying another organization or the development of an entirely new business line for the organization reside in the domain of this group. The skills needed at this level are more conceptual. What are the trends the organization needs to be concerned about? Where does the organization want to be in thirty years?

This overview of employee and leadership development points to several processes that are critical to the effectiveness of the organization.

These questions are major agenda items for the senior leadership team. If they are not, they should be. Put another way, the decisions and actions taken at the departmental level are primarily transactional in scope. The decisions and actions taken at the top of the organization are transformational in scope.

The introduction of COVID-19 has totally upended the apple cart, and some thoughtful consideration of the issue of employee management needs to occur. Working from home was to be a transitional stage. Work would eventually return to the office. This is certainly not the case, and many additional issues now confront the organization.

- Eight to five, five days a week is no longer acceptable to many employees. Why would I want to fight the traffic twice a day and have a boss watching my every move?
- Maybe I want to work part-time permanently?
- Maybe I will work two days a week in the office and then work from home the rest of the week.
- Fifteen dollars an hour? How about at least fifteen dollars an hour?
- The whole quest for a work-life balance has taken on an entirely new range of options.

It is too soon to forecast how this struggle will resolve itself. The number of business owners with extensive position openings suggest that this will not resolve itself any time soon. There will probably be a larger focus on the intrinsic rewards of work rather than the extrinsic.

The more strategic challenge facing the organization is the continued development of the workforce. The Society of Human Resources Management (SHRM) makes the distinction in career development in the following manner: (1) career planning and (2) career management. The individual employee is responsible for his or her career planning. The organization can promote this activity by making sure the issue of career planning is addressed in the annual review. Management is not to plan the career for the employee, but there is no reason why it cannot be asked about in the annual review. The second piece, career management, is clearly the responsibility of the organization to ensure it has the sustained and effective development of the organization's management and leadership ranks.

A further distinction is appropriate here: career development for the professional staff and career development for the management side of the house. In general, it is expected that the professional staff is well aware of the programs, workshops, institutes, etc. that will provide the appropriate advanced training needed to promote professional development. If they don't know, a goal for the new cycle would be to search and identify appropriate programs for the needed advancement. Career development for the management track is more complex.

There is a myriad amount of literature on the components of effective management and leadership. Attempting to choose the one best suited for you is a nonstarter. Begin with a candid and thorough examination of the leadership styles that have, historically, been successful in this organization. The organization does not want to promote only one style, exclusively, but narrowing the range a bit makes sense. On the other hand, are there common elements in terms of style and behavior that have not proved successful? Develop the profile of the typically successful leader and the profile of those who have proved unsuccessful. These two profiles should be carried forward for planning and selection purposes. They should not be relied on exclusively, but they should be viewed as one important piece of the puzzle.

There is no lack of training and development programs that are quick to assure an employer success if their candidate attends program X. The HR department, in collaboration with current managers and leaders, should develop a short list and then send managers to the approved list of programs. This should ensure the diversity typically sought in the leadership ranks.

The bottom line concerning all development planning is that it should not be ad hoc. Some commonsense analysis of what is and is not working in the organization regarding the professional and managerial development of employees is needed. Asking the question only when there is a position that needs to be filled ASAP will not suffice.

Termination/Separation

Sometimes, it may be determined that the organization has made the wrong employment decision and that, for the sake of both parties, it is best to terminate the employment relationship. That said, the process is anything but simple.

Case Study

As Emily prepared herself for the long drive home, she tightened her grip on the steering wheel, resisting the urge to veer left into oncoming traffic, resisting the urge to veer right sending herself plunging into the deep ravine. What would she tell her family? Termination.

Have you ever been terminated, eliminated, or separated from an organization? The very terminology implies something ominous is happening. Despair, isolation, even death. When you think about what the act signifies, feelings brought forth may be similar to those experienced when someone dies.

"Death is not the greatest loss in life. The greatest loss is what dies inside us while we live." Knowing what we know about death, the five stages of the grief cycle were first recognized and documented by Swiss psychiatrist Elisabeth Kubler-Ross in her internationally bestselling 1969 book titled *On Death and Dying*. The stages include Denial, Anger, Bargaining, Depression, and finally Acceptance/Hope. It is important to note that the grieving process is not linear, and not all stages will be experienced by all in the grieving population. Some may experience one, two, or three of the stages rather than all five. If the following illustration looks messy and unorganized, it is intended as such to give you an idea of the array and complexity of human emotions. Some may experience more than one stage at the same time. For example, as illustrated below, Anger and Depression are frequently experienced simultaneously, triggered by one

or the other. Most begin the process with denial and isolation and move between the stages, back and forth, up and down, skipping around until eventually they realize that hope for a new beginning is on the horizon. No two individuals will follow the same path.

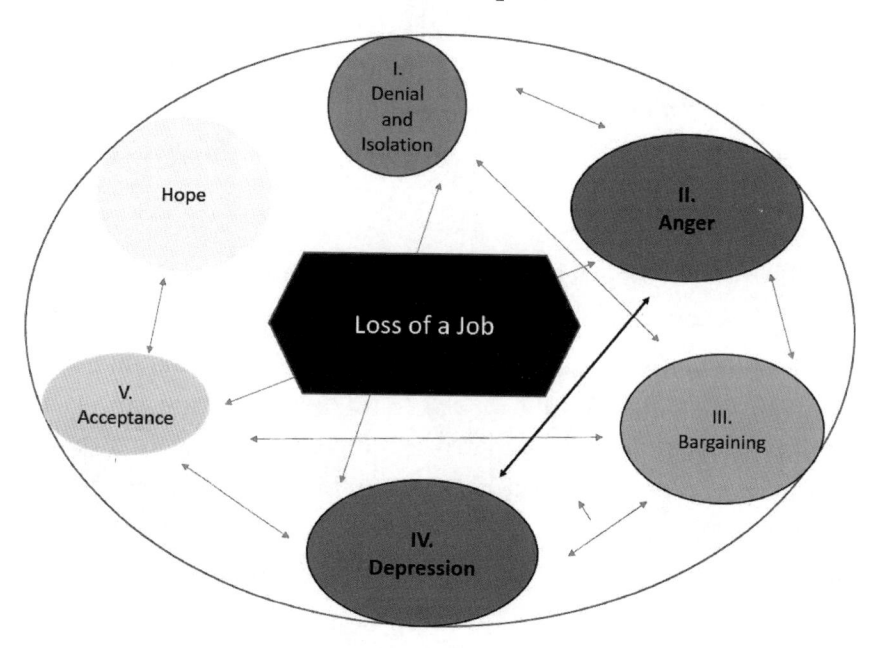

Diagram: Loss of a Job — I. Denial and Isolation, II. Anger, III. Bargaining, IV. Depression, V. Acceptance, Hope

Hearing the words "terminated" or "fired" may result in feelings of shock or disbelief even if the event was not totally unexpected by the recipient. This may trigger the first stage in the grief cycle, followed quickly by anger when the reality of the situation begins to settle in. It is important to realize that there is no standard timeline for each of the stages, and as a manager you must be prepared to react professionally to whatever type of outburst the employee may display. They might try to plead with you or offer some type of compromise in order to keep their job. When that doesn't work, they may become overwhelmed, act aggressively or exhibit hostile behavior. In any event, the job of the manager is to help them accept the situation and move on. This task is easier said than done, as portrayed in the 2009 motion picture *Up in the Air* starring George Clooney and Anna Kendrick. The premise of the movie is to demonstrate the importance of face-to-face meetings with those being fired. As important of a concept as this is, it is just the beginning.

Based on recent research conducted through social media in 2021, some common themes have emerged regarding what not to do in a termination meeting. The research participants in this study agreed to answer a series of questions. The stories they told, as described below, were both fascinating and horrifying at the same time. With consent, snippets from a few of their stories are being shared to better understand firsthand the negative effects of a termination meeting handled badly.

Joe: considers himself the luckiest guy in the world. Joe found himself in the termination meeting after four years of employment. He described the owner as having his entire identity tied up with the company. The owner did not keep up with the times in regard to technology, the internet, or email. The company was losing money, and the owner was looking for a scapegoat. Joe was summoned to the office, where he was subjected to a personal tirade having nothing to do with his job performance. So how does this make Joe "the luckiest guy in the world"? Life has a way of turning things around. More than fifteen years later, after several turnovers in management, Joe was hired back as CFO of the organization and is happily serving in that capacity today.

Mark: caught by surprise with no recourse. Mark was hired as a temporary employee to assist in conversion to a new system. When the temp role ended, the time was extended, and he was offered a job upon graduation—created and tailored for him. Four and a half years later, on a Friday afternoon, Mark found himself in the termination meeting. Earlier that day, Mark was told that a consultant had been hired to document how to do his job. In his mind, this made sense, as no one else knew how to run payroll or perform many of the other required tasks in the system. The day progressed as Mark explained each step of each process and the consultant took copious notes. Around 4 p.m., the director invited Mark to his office, where he found his immediate supervisor and a representative from Human Resources. The supervisor said that "they felt the need to part ways." HR offered no answers to any of his questions. A security guard watched Mark as he packed his boxes and walked him to his car. After six weeks of unemployment, Mark landed a new job with more flexibility and better pay. He has been with the organization of the "new" job for the past twenty-eight years.

Sharon: eliminated to make room for a friend of the vice president's secretary. There was a change in management at the organization where Sharon had worked for over ten years. The new vice president decided to eliminate thirty-one positions. Prior to the termination, Sharon had received an exceptional performance review and a bonus. On a Friday afternoon, her immediate supervisor called her into a conference room and left her there alone. A few minutes later, a representative from Human Resources came in, reviewed the severance policy, and walked her out the door "like a criminal." Sharon worked in HR and knew that there was nothing she could do about the situation. She was not surprised to learn that she was barred from ever going back into the building because that was the way these things were handled in HR. All her belongings were put into a box and mailed to her house. As a side note, one of Sharon's coworkers did not fare as well. Bob, a long-term employee of the company, had just had surgery and was on sick leave shortly after the new vice president took over. Sharon explained that HR went to Bob's house and fired him. She said it was "absolutely horrible" and a terrible way to treat people who had shown loyalty. When word of Bob's and the others' stories spread, it caused huge public relations issues for the company.

Different people, different scenarios, same results. Some individuals may feel discomfort even reading the stories. Beliefs are formed based on life experiences, many with long-term effects causing the individual to feel that they may never be successful or get another job.

Below you will find some suggestions to help managers mitigate the situation and improve the outcome of the termination meeting.

(1) It is personal. Most importantly, a manager needs to communicate honestly with his or her staff on a daily basis. No employee should ever be blindsided regarding expectations or aspects of their performance. Once the decision has been made, allow the employee to maintain their dignity. Do not rehash errors or negative situations that have previously been discussed. Keep it short and to the point: "We are taking different paths." Thinking back to an annual performance meeting in my distant past, when I asked what I could do to improve my performance, I was told "Nothing." Great, I thought, until she continued with, "I think it is just your personality." Yikes! That was over fifteen years ago, and I remember it like it was yesterday. It is very personal.

(2) Choose the right time of day. Early morning is usually best. While late afternoon may be the most convenient time for the manager, from the employee's perspective, it doesn't seem fair to expect someone to work all day and let them go after a full shift. A face-to-face conversation, in a private location, is preferable. If face-to-face or mask-to-mask contact is impossible due to restrictions and protocols related to the COVID-19 pandemic, schedule an on-camera meeting as a last resort. Be sure to convey empathy in speech and facial expression.

(3) Prepare a list of talking points and stick to the script. Know in advance what will be said to the individual and what is planned to be said to coworkers and team members. Keep the message as positive, yet neutral, as possible. Practice how to handle the uncomfortable conversation and difficult questions. Check your verbal communication skills and body language. Choose your words carefully but know that at some point the recipient of the bad news will most likely stop listening, tune out, and revert to preconceived notions. Much like receiving a bad diagnosis at the doctor's office, actions speak louder than words. Remember, terminations, and in particular the way they are handled, can cause ongoing PR problems for the organization long after the employee has

"taken a different path." Surviving employees may also lose their sense of security and fear for their own prospects of a future with the company.

(4) Enlist the help of professionals. If feasible, offer outplacement services. Have a representative on-site and available to talk about career transition and what to expect. These experts are trained and comfortable dealing with employees who suddenly find themselves in this situation. Provide contact information with phone numbers to benefits specialists, including where to find information on COBRA, applicable severance packages, and unemployment benefits.

As for Emily, she was not an individual who had tied her entire identity to her job and title. However, she did experience a loss of income, loss of self-esteem, and many of the stages of grief including anger and depression. Her social circle dwindled as former coworkers called less and less frequently. Making new friends seemed more difficult. The question "What do you do?" and the answer "I am in-between jobs right now" did not invite additional conversation or spark a warm and fuzzy feeling for anyone, especially for those who have felt the hopelessness and abandonment of a similar situation.

The long-lasting effects of a termination can be life-shattering. For optimal success, treat each individual with respect by taking the time to prepare for the unexpected and conduct the discussion with compassion, integrity, and kindness. Remember, every human life is unique, irreplaceable, and deserving of respect. People may not remember exactly what was said, but they will remember how it made them feel.

One last thought: always double check the spelling of names and attach the employee identification number to make sure the right person is called into the termination meeting. In my research, I came across an individual who shared an interesting story to illustrate this point. With a common name like Laura Smith, one might expect many cases of mistaken identity. This was the case when Laura received a call from HR and was told to meet her supervisor in the conference room, as she was being fired. As Laura pulled together all her strength to stand up from her desk and make her way down the hall, the phone rang again. Yes, it was HR, and there had been a mistake. The call was made to the wrong Laura Smith. Her response: "Way to give a fat girl a heart attack."

Change Management (Transactional)

Implicit in much of the discussion to this point is the fact that the HR department is constantly changing as its agenda and goals change in a highly uncertain environment. Change can be dictated at the departmental level, at the group level, and at the organizational level.

You may find it helpful to review the introduction of systems theory found on pages 53–57. The basic model is detailed there. The actual archetype discussed there is more transformational. The archetype suggested by Senge to illustrate transformational change is labeled "Fixes That Fail." The same technique is used here but the chosen archetypes are more transactional. The first archetype is found below.

CONCERNED WORKERS

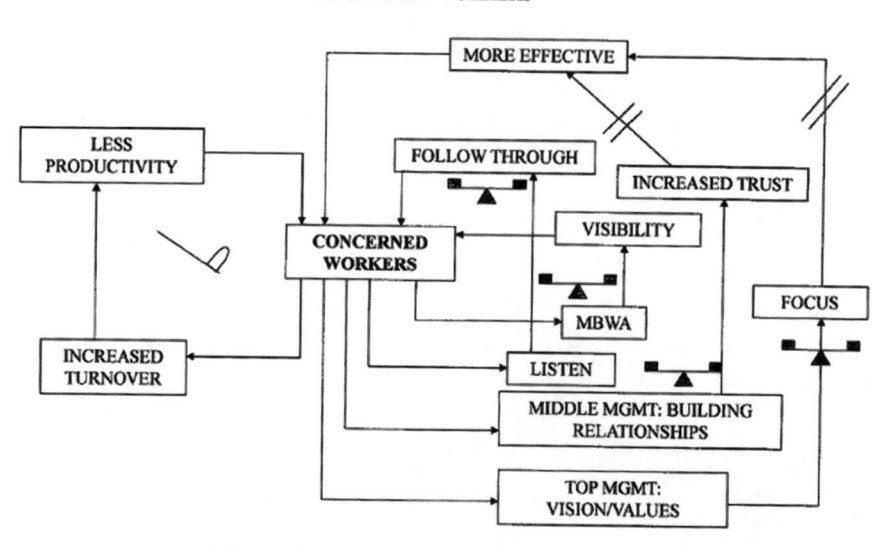

[Diagram: A systems archetype diagram showing relationships between CONCERNED WORKERS (center), LESS PRODUCTIVITY, INCREASED TURNOVER, MORE EFFECTIVE, FOLLOW THROUGH, INCREASED TRUST, VISIBILITY, MBWA, LISTEN, FOCUS, MIDDLE MGMT: BUILDING RELATIONSHIPS, and TOP MGMT: VISION/VALUES.]

This archetype begins at the center of the graph with the box labeled "Concerned Workers." Workers can be concerned about many factors within the organization. To illustrate this archetype, we consider the concerns to be the result of the employees' fear that the organization is decreasing in viability. The factors that lead to this concern are not important at this point. The loop to the left illustrates the typical response of the employee in this instance. You can expect that the concerned employee will begin to look for a new job if this causal link is correct. You would expect to see the employee dusting off his or her resume and making sure that the resume is on LinkedIn. The employee might ask his or her colleagues to be on the lookout for a new job for him or her. This is the beginning of an accelerating loop. You can ask the question: what employee leaves the organization first?

If the marginal employee leaves first, this is probably good for all. However, more than likely, the employee that leaves first is the one that is most attractive to other organizations in the marketplace. In other words, the best employees leave first because they are the ones that have the skills, experience, and know-how that are most attractive in the marketplace. The result of this activity is that the organization experiences a continually decreasing level of productivity if this process continues. As the organization becomes even less productive, this process further enhances the concern on the part of those employees still within the firm. They now experience the classical accelerating loop: concern leads to increased turnover leads to less productivity leads to more concern.

The organization is looped. A possible remedy would be to increase the level of salary for the employees. This is probably a short-term fix. First of all, the organization probably lacks the resources to increase the salary of the employees. Second, while there is an initial positive impact if the increase in salary is implemented, the employee quickly forgets about the increase and the firm is back where it started. Suffice it to say this is not a good strategy or alternative. The question continues to confront management of what to do about this accelerating loop.

More effective responses on the part of the organization appear to the right in the archetype. Four are offered here for illustration. First, top management can become more aggressive in determining its strategic plan. It may consider its vision in the face of environmental conditions and further clarify the values that it holds near and dear. What may result from this effort is a more rigorous and hopefully achievable strategic plan with goals and resources and timetables attached. If this is the result of the strategic planning effort by top management, the organization will then have a better focus as to what has to happen in the day-in and day-out activity of that organization. This particular result, it is argued, will make the organization more effective, and if the firm is more effective in the marketplace the result is that the concern exhibited by workers will go down because they see a better light at the end of the tunnel. Notice that there are two hash marks between "focus" and "more effective" once an organization develops its strategic plan. It cannot execute or see that execution to fruition immediately. It takes time; hence the hash marks represent the delay between the delineation of the plan and its execution.

Put another way, there are concerned workers. Management develops a clear strategic plan that is communicated throughout the organization. The organization becomes more effective because it focuses on its plan and eventually the worker becomes less concerned. This loop is a balancing loop and is indicated by the seesaw found just below the box labeled "focus."

Note the second balancing loop. When an organization is experiencing significant dysfunction, middle management tends to concern itself with its own departmental members. Each middle manager circles the wagons to maintain his or her own employees. Efforts involving working across departments are minimized. It is more important to focus on one's current team. As a possible remedy to this situation, the second balancing loop initiates training among the middle management to further develop middle management relationships. What might be an effective contributing factor would be to initiate a training program among middle management that is focused on rebuilding the relations among departmental managers.

This effort should focus on the role that middle management plays in the accomplishment of overall goals and on ensuring that the activities responsible for this execution are effective and in place. If this building relationships program is effective, it is argued here that this will increase the level of trust among middle managers and that will also contribute to a more effective firm. Again, the delay hashtags are present because this is not accomplished overnight.

The third balancing loop is to send the chief executive officer out to press the flesh and to improve the communication between managers and employees. It is argued here that the senior management, in this instance the CEO, needs to listen more effectively to the employees and then follow through as appropriate. This again will delay or reduce the concern on the part of workers. A final balancing loop is delineated by MBWA. This stands for "management by walking around." It is argued here that if senior management is more visible to the people in the organization, this will have a positive impact on the employees.

So what is illustrated here are four balancing loops that, in the aggregate, provide both strategic and operational processes that are focused on increasing the effectiveness of the organization and decreasing the concern on the part of the employees. What makes this process so complicated is the fact that the employees, particularly the concerned employees, are in the church of what is happening now. Their timeline is short: three to six months. The balancing loops illustrated in this graph, however, may take three to five years to execute and bear fruit in the organization. The firm may not have that long before the loss of important employees further dooms the organization.

Here is another fully developed transactional archetype to illustrate how this process works.

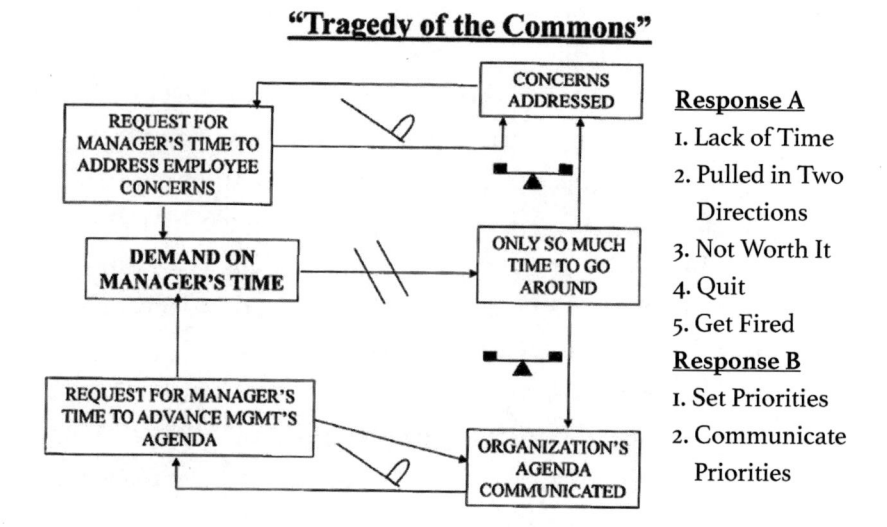

"Tragedy of the Commons"

Response A
1. Lack of Time
2. Pulled in Two Directions
3. Not Worth It
4. Quit
5. Get Fired

Response B
1. Set Priorities
2. Communicate Priorities

The Tragedy of the Commons goes like this:

1. Time is a scarce resource for all employees and especially for middle managers, as this archetype illustrates.
2. At the top of the archetype, a subordinate seeks out his or her superior and solicits assistance in addressing a particular problem. The manager listens to the situation and then provides a solution. If the problem is resolved effectively, there is the beginning of an accelerating loop. The next time the subordinate encounters a problem, he or she will return to the manager in the hope that effective aid will be forthcoming again. Word spreads among the subordinates about the capacity of the middle manager, and the scarce time of the manager is further compromised.
3. The middle manager is also sought out by senior management to present various action plans to the workers. The workers are known to trust this middle manager. The result is that another accelerating loop is further developed. Top management will be back with another action plan to be introduced later.

4. The middle manager also has certain tasks that are part of his or her responsibilities. If the current situation continues, subordinates and top management will consume all the discretionary time of the middle manager, and his or her performance will suffer.
5. Simple strategies may assist (Response B). First, set priorities and schedule the time necessary to meet these priorities ASAP. Second, shut the door and communicate to all that, when the door is shut, the manager is not available.
6. Failure to set these priorities and act accordingly (Response A) will lead to burnout as the manager attempts to meet all demands. The result will be burnout and maybe even quitting the position.
7. If the middle manager does not burn out, he or she may eventually be fired because his or her job responsibilities are not being accomplished.
8. The tragedy of the commons is that the time of the middle manager is consumed by all parties and the organization loses this essential resource in the process.

These two archetypes illustrate the transactional nature of change. They tend to focus on individuals rather than the organization and illustrate the problems that emerge at a more transactional level.

Now, turn back to page 52 of the text and review the Burke model. Two additional observations are noted. First, the twelve factors included in the Burke model provide a good balance among factors needed to be considered as you initiate the change process. Some of the factors are macro and consider the organization as a whole.

External Environment
Mission and Strategy
Leadership
Organizational Culture

Others look at internal processes that are operative within the organization.

Structure
Management practices
Systems
Work Unit Climate

The third set of factors focuses on the individual employee and his or her performance in that organization.

Task requirements and individual skills
Motivation
Individual Needs and Values
Individual, Group, and Organizational Performance

The second reality to consider is the interactive nature that exists in this model. Each factor is substantially related to other factors within the model. Therefore, it is imperative that the change agent not only notes the impact of changes to the factor being addressed but also gives full consideration to the impact on the other factors that are related to that initial factor. Failure to do this important analysis will lead to ineffective change outcomes.

To improve the quality of information available to the organizational decision-makers, it is highly recommended that primary data be collected on a regular basis. The model provided by Burke indicates the factors that you need to consider. Provided below is an assessment tool that provides three items for each of the twelve factors in the Burke model. Therefore, the complete survey would provide data across thirty-six items for consideration on the part of decision-makers. If the organization employs the assessment tool on a regular basis, the decision-makers will note trends in the information regarding what is and is not working within the organization. The twelve factors provided by the Burke model are foundational. The actual items that assess performance in each of those twelve factors are open to the discretion of the organizational decision-makers. The actual items can be changed, but once changed it is imperative that the same assessment tool be used in further administrations of the assessment so that decision-makers are comparing apples to apples and oranges to oranges. Failure to operate carefully in this avenue produces the typical scenario: garbage in, garbage out.

COMPANY X

MANAGEMENT AND CHANGE ASSESSMENT

EXTERNAL ENVIRONMENT

1. The external business environment is very dynamic for COMPANY X
2. The population feels COMPANY X is delivering high quality products and services.
3. COMPANY X is responding effectively to the current business environment

MISSION AND STRATEGY

1. The mission and strategy of COMPANY X are carefully designed to meet the challenges of the current and future business environment
2. The mission and strategy are clearly understood by the employees of COMPANY X
3. The mission and strategy are assessed and updated on a regular basis

ORGANIZATION CULTURE

1. The values of COMPANY X are clearly evident in the behavior of its employees
2. The values of COMPANY X are regularly communicated to all employees
3. The values guide the determination of policies and procedures for COMPANY X

LEADERSHIP

1. Senior leadership continually provides a clear vision and direction for COMPANY X
2. Senior leadership provides an excellent role model for those who eventually will occupy these positions
3. Leadership is exercised through careful deliberation and appropriate persuasion

STRUCTURE

1. The arrangement of functional areas and departments effectively contribute to getting the work done
2. Levels of responsibility, decision-making authority, and lines of communication effectively support the accomplishment of COMPANY X goals
3. Senior management regularly reviews and changes the structure, as warranted, to accomplish COMPANY X goals

MANAGEMENT PRACTICES

1. Middle management practices encourage employees to take initiative regarding innovative approaches to various tasks and projects
2. Middle managers are generally competent in their management practices
3. Middle managers receive clear guidance regarding their roles and responsibilities through management development programs and mentoring from their superiors

POLICIES AND PROCEDURES

1. Policies and procedures are carefully designed and communicated to employees
2. Policies and procedures are designed to help employees with their job roles and responsibilities
3. Policies and procedures provide helpful guidance for coordinating work and decision making across units

WORK UNIT CLIMATE

1. Employees are clear about what is expected of them in their jobs
2. Employees feel their performance is recognized
3. Employees feel they are managed according to standards that are challenging and fair

MOTIVATION

1. Employees feel they can exercise reasonable autonomy on the job
2. Employees feel they have the appropriate tools to do their job
3. Employees are generally satisfied with the rewards they receive for their work

TASK REQUIREMENTS AND INDIVIDUAL SKILLS / ABILITIES

1. Employees are hired with the appropriate abilities and skills to do their jobs
2. Employees are offered appropriate training and development opportunities for career advancement
3. Employees feel there are reasonable career paths for advancement in the organization

INDIVIDUAL NEEDS AND VALUES

1. Employees feel their individual needs are met when working within COMPANY X
2. The values employees hold closely are consistently supported in their work
3. The values of the employees and of COMPANY X are closely aligned

INDIVIDUAL AND ORGANIZATIONAL PERFORMANCE

1. The quality of business outcomes provided by COMPANY X is excellent
2. COMPANY X is a very innovative organization
3. COMPANY X is accurately characterized as a learning organization

MEASUREMENT SCALE

STRONGLY DISAGREE						STRONGLY AGREE
1	2	3	4	5	6	7

If your organization collects information like this on an annual basis, you are in a position to compare across administrations of the survey and note what is going well and where things need to be improved. You may also change the items and/or add additional factors deemed important to the organization.

Case Study

To illustrate the relevancy of this, consider your interaction with the banking industry today. As an example, what happens if your current password does not work? You may be lucky enough to follow the prompts and change the password. If this remedy does not work, you will probably have to call a phone number. This is when the process really goes awry. The typical wait time to get a real person on the line is somewhere between fifteen and twenty-five minutes. You will be peppered with interruptions thanking you for your patience and assuring you that you are a valued customer. For this bank customer, all that results is further aggravation.

When the bank representative finally comes on the line, ask the representative if senior management has ever asked for his or her opinion as to how customers are feeling in the trenches. That question results in a very halting response. One might conclude the halt is precipitated by the fact that that question does not occur on the script that the representative is provided. It is not worth the effort to chew out the representative on the phone because he or she has no power to make change. You may be provided a survey after the interview, but my experience indicates the total lack of the opportunity to express my true feelings on the issues that I think are important regarding the interaction and/or my opinion of how the bank is doing to meet my needs. You are left with the feeling that top management either is not receiving good information about what is happening in the trenches or could care less about what is happening in the trenches (or both). You are now heading down the proverbial rabbit hole.

None of the factors noted in the Burke model will assess the frustration experienced by the customer in the case study. In this instance, the bank may employ additional information gathering techniques. Non-directive questioning found in a focus group with current customers is but one example.

In general, thoughtful people conclude that change at any level in the firm is typically met with levels of resistance. As you move up the levels of the organization, change involves more of the factors operative within the organization, and that further results in the negative consequences associated with change.

In summary, change is not the easiest course of action for individuals and organizations. Often, employees and the organization actively resist change. In this instance, the path of an evolutionary change process is not available. Small incremental changes may have successfully resolved the problem, but they are not considered. The situation worsens and then a revolutionary change is needed to address the problem. Welcome to the change process.

Why is this discussion on organizational change relevant to the HR department? David Ulrich argues that the effective HR department is tasked with four roles. They are noted in the following table.

BUSINESS PARTNER	CHANGE AGENT
ADMINISTRATIVE EXPERT	EMPLOYEE CHAMPION

Activities associated with the "Administrative Expert" role are typically maintenance activities. Keeping track of vacations, revising the HR policy manual, and talking to employees about their health benefits are important but transactional in scope.

The other three roles are strategic. If the HR department is to provide value added to the firm, it needs to speak for the legitimate needs of the employee and then become an effective *coordinator* of the change process for the organization. If HR accomplishes these two roles successfully, rest assured that HR will find a significant place at the table and be recognized as an essential business partner.

Organizations come in many sizes and shapes. The accelerating loop discussed in this section is applicable to both ends of the spectrum: small and large. When the organization finds itself in the initial start-up phase, the substantial risk is finding the individuals who will take the high risk and plunder into the unknown. When the organization has matured and gained size, the challenge is to guard against the bureaucratic structure that takes over. However, regardless of size, the accelerating loop discussed in this section still holds.

When implementing any change, the eight steps of John Kotter provide a solid guide. They are listed below.

- A sense of urgency: tension in the system is a strong foundation for calling for change.
- A guiding coalition: a committed team of individuals who are coordinating the change effort is needed.
- A strategic vision: we need to know where we are going.
- A volunteer army: we need followers at all levels who are committed to the changes.
- Action by removing barriers: change without obstacles is tough enough. Remove obvious obstacles.
- Short-term wins: leaders need to point to successes along the way and celebrate them.
- Acceleration: effective change should accelerate the change process.
- Change: the only constant these days is change. Get used to it.

CONCLUSION

If you have gotten to this point, you now appreciate why management is more difficult than rocket science. General management and human resources management are essential and challenging activities for the leadership team that seeks to achieve consistent and sustainable growth. This book does not provide all the answers. It does provide an overview of the essential management activities and provides an approach that makes ample use of the following:

1. A systems perspective that stresses the "looped" nature of organization life and the challenges this perspective provides for understanding what is occurring in the department or organization. More important, the perspective offers ways you might proceed to resolve the issues you face.
2. Management models (theories), when integrated into your thinking about how to be an effective member of the general management team or a member of the HR staff, enhance the strategies and solutions you develop and implement in developing answers to the challenges currently faced by management.

Below are four cases that illustrate the relevancy and value of the models developed throughout this book. The source for the first three cases is the *Wall Street Journal* during the week of February 6, 2023. The fourth case is reported in the *St. Louis Post Dispatch* during the same week.

Elon Musk February 6, 2023
Elon Musk is a billionaire entrepreneur who has been very successful in the development of Tesla and SpaceX and is now tackling the challenges

found in Twitter. Tesla and SpaceX are primarily engineering ventures while Twitter is more of a retail operation.

Twitter was founded in 2007 and by 2017 it had 330 million monthly users. It employs 4,900 employees and has a market capitalization of 32.577 billion. Five hundred million tweets are executed daily. Its substantial growth has brought significant attention from the federal government and plenty of questions regarding the use of the service from many corners of its retail users.

The cost to Mr. Musk personally has been significant. He describes himself as a nano manager who now suffers from significant back pain. Before acquiring Twitter, his work week was eighty hours a week. With the purchase of Twitter, his work week has exploded to 120 hours.

Zoom February 8, 2023

Zoom is laying off 1,300 employees or 15 percent of its staff. Substantial growth occurred during the pandemic-fueled spurt caused by COVID-19.

Eric Yuan, the CEO, stated "we didn't take as much time as we should have to thoroughly analyze our teams or assess if we were growing sustainably, toward the highest priorities."

Mr. Yuan is reducing his salary 98 percent in the coming fiscal year and not taking his 2023 bonus. Members of his team will take a 20 percent cut in pay and forego 2023 corporate bonuses.

Boeing February 8, 2023

It will cut 2,000 jobs in finance and human resources. The company will hire 10,000 jobs primarily in engineering and manufacturing. Future efforts will include simplifying its corporate structure.

The Archdiocese of St. Louis

Full disclosure: I am a member of one of the parishes that is slated for closing.

The Archdiocese of St. Louis is implementing a plan to reduce the number of parishes, 176 in total, to 88 pastorates. The final announcement of the parish reductions will occur on Pentecost Sunday, 2023.

Two-hour listening sessions have been conducted in each parish. These sessions have included a video featuring the Vicar of Strategic Planning, who provided an overview of the program. The session included a presentation of the tentative clustering of the existent parishes. The programs were moderated by lay volunteers. Some time was provided for questions, observations, and answers from those in attendance.

The number of active priests in the archdiocese is approximately 190. The average age is approximately sixty-five.

The four cases noted above are certainly more complex than indicated in these short overviews and the solutions are more complex than will be developed below. The goal here is to illustrate how the content of this book can be applied to provide a path for decision-makers tasked with resolving these challenges.

Twitter

The Twitter mission statement reads "We serve the public conversation." The mission statement is supported by seven values including: promoting health; earning trust of people; uniting purpose and profits; being free, fast, and fun; making it simply straightforward; and sustainability and environmental conservation.

Observation: these provide a very good twenty-thousand-foot perspective but there is much to be done to show how these operate at the ten-foot level. Substantial effort is needed to make this mission statement operable on a daily level.

Mr. Musk is spending 120 hours a week managing his vast network of businesses. This pace is not sustainable. The CEO of the firm is a key determinant of the stability of the enterprise. The health of this individual is important. A heart attack is not good.

The archetype "Fixes That Fail" provides some guidance here. Mr. Musk's takeover of the firm is revolutionary. One of his first moves was to initiate a reduction in force which further created turmoil among employees. It also creates a wait-and-see posture among employees who are wondering when the next shoe will fall. They assume a wait-and-see attitude.

Mr. Musk cannot lead the charge for change as a single individual. He needs the senior management team to assist in the transition. The goal is to develop an effective senior management team that is ready and willing to take on the key challenges the organization faces. This process will not occur quickly. It may take twelve months to have an operating senior management team and the strategic plan may take years to implement. Patience!

Zoom

Observation: Mr. Yuan's observation is right on target. Zoom needs to carefully analyze its team and assess its plans to grow sustainably. The substantial reduction of annual salary and bonuses focused on Mr. Yuan and the senior management team demonstrates accountability focused on those responsible for the strategic planning efforts.

The strategic planning process will create delays as the firm develops effective structures to meet future challenges. There will be further delays experienced in the plan implementation and the manifestation of expected outcomes.

Boeing

Observation: more information is needed regarding the cut in human resources capacity. If the goal is to simplify the corporate structure, the human resources team is frequently critical to this process. David Ulrich argues for four key responsibilities for human resources. Two of these are business partner and change management. If the cuts represent a reduction in capacity regarding administrative duties, fine.

If the cuts are focused on the more strategic activities of the human resources department, there will be more problems.

Archdiocese of St. Louis

The focus here is on the management of the process, not religion directly. The number of people participating in religious practices in traditional Christian religions has been experiencing a gradual decline over the past decades in the United States and the decline in church attendance among Catholics is consistent with this trend.

The efforts of the St Louis archdiocese are focused on the local level. The Catholic church, in general, has been very slow to change. Vatican Two is the source of many changes in the church but some key changes have not emerged. Two of these changes are the introduction of married clergy and the ordination of women. Both of this would probably alleviate some of the challenges the church faces today. They would also create new problems. Neither of these are under local diocesan control.

Two observations are noted in this change process at the local level. The first is the archdiocese has chosen the number of participants that are expected to be in the new arrangements as the key measure dictating the designation of the pastorates. The second is the decision to announce the changes for the entire diocese all at once. A change of this magnitude requires significant support systems. The disruption of the individual communities in each parish will be significant. Executing the change in a portion of the diocese would lessen the expected turmoil and provide the degrees of freedom to learn and execute further changes with less problems.

The change process employed here, while not strategic, would benefit from greater communication and less disruption.

Make no mistake, effective management takes practice over the long run. Failure is an opportunity to grow. You will fail many times. The question is whether you stand up, dust off, and try again.

So what do you need to bring to the table if you wish to be successful?

- Integrity is always at the top of the list. Yes, there are plenty of examples of leaders who are in leadership positions who lack integrity, but they do not engender true commitment among their followers.
- Be an exceptional listener. You may learn something, and you are showing respect to another individual.
- Remember that management is a team sport. The environment and the challenges it generates are rarely resolved by one individual. It is a team that gets it done.
- Do not be afraid to make a decision. The world is full of Monday morning quarterbacks.
- Be informed. Choose a few trusted sources of information that cut across all perspectives.
- Have a good sense of humor. Start by being willing to laugh at yourself.
- Have a plan. Don't be constrained by what you think needs to be in the plan. You will change the plan on a regular basis. That is good and healthy. No plan leads to ineffective activity. You do not need to boil the ocean. Pick your patch and be good at understanding that patch and managing it. Do that well and others will give you more opportunities to manage additional patches.
- Have fun in the process. Those who think they can do better, can't.

Glossary

Limits To Growth

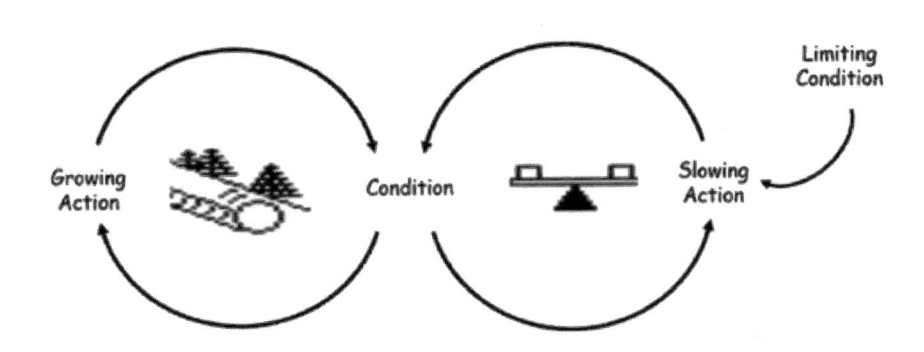

- Growing Action → Condition → Slowing Action ← Limiting Condition

Tragedy of the Commons

- Individual A's Activity → Net Gains for A → Individual A's Activity
- Individual B's Activity → Net Gains for B → Individual B's Activity
- Total Activity —Delay→ Gain per Individual Activity ← Resource Limit

113

Fixes That Fail

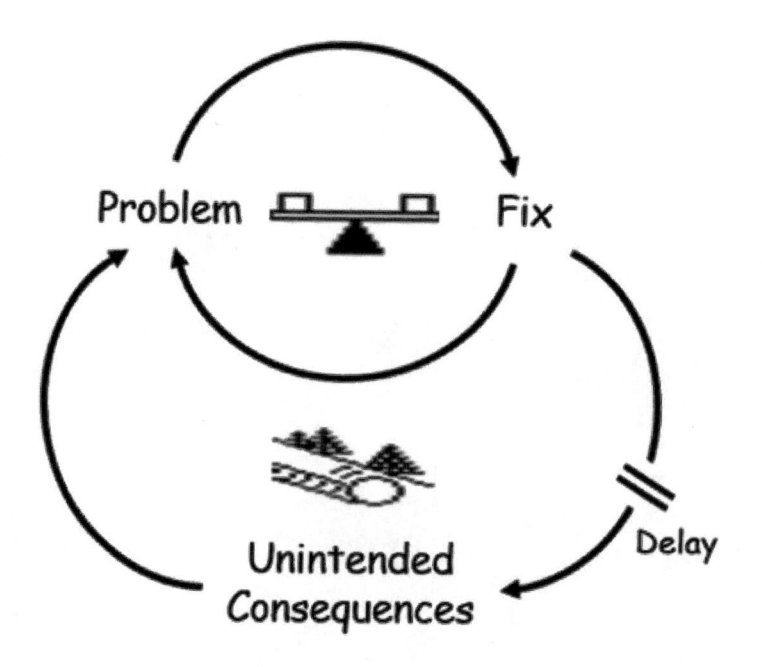

Problem ⚖ Fix

Unintended Consequences

Delay

Acknowledgments

My fellow contributors to the manuscript are critical for their knowledge and insight into these topics, but without their continual support throughout this endeavor we would have never accomplished the publication of this book.

Permissions

Jon Pierce and Donald Gardner, *Management and Organizational Behavior: An Integrated Perspective*, 2002, South-Western, p. 387.

Victor Vroom and Philip Yetton, *Leadership and Decision-Making*, University of Pittsburgh Press, 1973, p.39

W. Warner Burke, *Organization Change Theory and Practice*, 2018, Sage Publications, Inc, p. 227

Peter Senge, *The Fifth Discipline, 1990*, Doubleday/Currency, New York, pp. 379, 387, 388

Bibliography

Adams, J. S., and S. Freedman. "Equity theory revisited: Comments and annotated bibliography." In *Equity Theory: Toward a General Theory of Social Interaction*, ed. Leonard Berkowitz and Elaine Walster, 43–90. Vol. 9 of *Advances in Experimental Social Psychology*. Academic Press, 1976.

Burke, W. Warner. *Organizational Change: Theory and Practice*. Thousand Oaks, CA: Sage, 2017.

Deci, Edward. *Self-Determination Theory: Basic Psychological Needs" in Motivation, Development, and Wellness*. Guilford Press, 2018.

Hambrick, Donald C. and James W. Fredrickson. "Are You Sure You Have a Strategy?" *The Academy of Management Executive* 15, no. 4 (Nov. 2001).

Kotter, John P. "Leading Change: Why Transformation Efforts Fail." *Harvard Business Review, 73(2), 59–67.*

Lindblom, C. E. "The Science of Muddling Through." *Public Administration Review* 19, 79–88.

Locke, Edwin and Gary P. Latham. *Goal Setting: A Motivational Technique That Works!* 1984.

Pierce, J. L., and Donald Gardner. *Management and Organizational Behavior*. Cincinnati: South-Western, 2001.

Rooke, David and William Torbert. "7 Transformations of Leadership." *Harvard Business Review*, April 2005, 66–76.

Eisenhower Decision-Making Model, found in Covey, Steven. *The 7 Habits of Highly Effective People.*

Senge, Peter. *The Fifth Discipline: The Art and Practice of the Learning Organization*. New York: Doubleday, 1990.

Tulgan, Bruce. *It's Okay to Be the Boss: The Step-by-Step Guide to Becoming the Manager Your Employees Need*, Harper-Collins, 2007

Ulrich, David. *Human Resource Champions.* Cambridge, MA: Harvard Business Review Press, 1996.

Vroom, Victor H. *Work and Motivation.* New York: Wiley, 1964

Vroom, Victor and P. W. Yetton. *Leadership and Decision-Making.* Pittsburgh: University of Pittsburgh Press, 1973.